The Small Shrub Garden

The
Small Shrub Garden

JUDITH M. BERRISFORD

FABER AND FABER
3 Queen Square
London

First published in 1961
by Faber and Faber Limited
3 Queen Square London WC1
New and revised edition 1975
Printed in Great Britain by
Unwin Brothers Limited
The Gresham Press
Old Woking, Surrey
All rights reserved

ISBN 0 571 10738 9 (Faber Paperbacks)
ISBN 0 571 04863 3 (hard bound edition)

For Cliff, who made the garden

Acknowledgements

I should like to acknowledge my gratitude to Mr.
Graham Thomas, Gardens Adviser to the National
Trust, and leading shrub-rose authority, for so kindly
checking the chapter on shrub roses and for his advice
thereon, and to Mr. Charles Puddle, Head Gardener to
Lord Aberconway and the National Trust at Bodnant,
and member of the Rhododendron and Camellia
committee of the Royal Horticultural Society, for his
help and guidance in the choice of camellias mentioned
in this book.

J. M. B.

Contents

CONTENTS

Illustrations

11

ILLUSTRATIONS

I

Shrub-Garden Scheme

Most of us think of shrub gardens in terms of several-acre estates. Yet shrubs may be used in small gardens with as good effect as in large. In fact, they are more than ever necessary in the small garden if any sort of character or distinction is to be obtained. From the sixty-by-thirty-foot plot behind the small suburban house, to the country half-acre or acre—any garden can be rendered more effective by the proper use of shrubs.

Shrubs and trees are the backbone of the garden. They give it permanent form and shape. In the winter, a garden which relies for its appeal upon bedding-plants, flower borders, or the conventional tea or floribunda roses, is bare. The herbaceous border is a sorry stubble, the rose bed a desolation, but the well-planned shrub garden with its skeleton of evergreens, and carpets of heaths, helianthemums (rock roses), or dwarf azaleas, is tidy and full of form. Such a garden will have winter colour—the scented gold of witch hazel—rosy-red and white *Erica carnea* varieties—cloudy pink autumn cherry—as well as the soft lilac of *Iris unguicularis*, and the speckled, mystic bowls of the hellebores; for even in a shrub garden the select few herbaceous plants have their appointed place.

In some people's minds a shrub garden may be synonymous with an informal, and perhaps untidy, garden, but shrub gardens may be either formal or informal, and they need never be untidy.

Properly carried out—the ground clothed by suitable dwarf evergreens—a shrub-garden scheme is the neatest of all, and it will always have a show of colour. Compare the effect of the odd clump of lupins, a wind-blown delphinium or two, and the few campanulas that are often all the small flower border can show at one season, with the blaze of glory that is a rhododendron in bloom. Moreover, the individual shrubs need never be too big for even the smallest garden. There are miniature rhododendrons, small-growers, and medium-sized varieties, just as there are different varieties of rose, berberis, mock orange, and other popular shrubs. Species or varieties can be found to suit gardens of any size.

When one thinks of rhododendrons these days one may immediately discard the dark leafed, weighty bushes of the public parks. The dwarf rhododendron 'Blue Tit' with neat half-inch leaves becomes in flower a mound of harebell-blue. The newer 'Sapphire' is even better. Both are hardy as heather and make compact bushes seldom more than two and a half to three feet in height.

This is the age of the small garden, and shrub gardening is the form of gardening most suited to its limited size. In such small space one wants only the best and one wants the garden always to look its best. This is possible only with shrubs and trees to form sweeping lines; with neat carpeting growth in the foreground and the contrasting spires and mounds of suitable evergreens to form a framework that is pleasing the year round. Deciduous shrubs play their part but they should be so placed that the eye may be led past them to a mass of attractive evergreen foliage when they are out of flower. Bulbs and herbaceous treasures are tucked into bays where they may be easily tended. A shrub garden can appeal to the house-proud and tidy-minded more than any other garden. Wisely planted it has no off-season—it is always at its best, winter summer, autumn, spring—there is always interest and colour. Some shrub or tree is always in flower and it is in the appreciation of form and individual blossom that most of us find the greatest joy.

My plan in this book is to show how shrubs may satisfactorily be used as the main ingredients in the design of a small garden and to suggest suitable shrubs for such a scheme, taking each season in turn.

Where a particular variety or species is mentioned for the first time, the size it may be expected to reach ten years from planting will be given in parentheses after its name. The size will be given in feet, the height being mentioned first and then the spread. A complete list of shrubs and trees mentioned, grouped according to size, and with a note as to their flowering time and whether they are evergreen or deciduous, will be given at the end of the book. The given size should be taken merely as a guide to the space required when planting and not as a definite prediction. With good cultivation in an average garden the shrubs should attain the stated proportions in the allotted time. In heavily shaded gardens with an overhead canopy of forest trees the shrubs will grow taller because they will be drawn up to seek the light. In poor soil, in frost-hollows, or in gardens exposed to biting winds they will probably not reach their given size. Except where specifically stated the shrubs and trees mentioned are hardy under normal conditions throughout the British Isles.

Because a shrub that measures only two-feet-six in height by a foot in width when first planted may in ten years' time become six feet high with a spread of five it is necessary to plant such trees and shrubs as are to form part of the permanent garden design at the spacing necessary to accommodate their ultimate growth. This will result in the newly planted garden having a sparse aspect which may be counteracted by interplanting with cheaper, quick-growing shrubs which may easily be removed as the permanent occupants fill out and require their spaces. Tree lupins, brooms, the hardier veronicas, and *Lavatera olbia* 'Rosea', the tree mallow, are ideal for such a purpose together with some of the more robust herbaceous plants—campanulas, irises, aquilegias, paeonies, and foxgloves.

Rhododendrons (including azaleas) and shrub roses are perhaps the two genera which have most to offer the shrub gardener and so I have allotted each of these a chapter to itself. Rhododendrons will be found in Chapter 8 and Shrub Roses in Chapter 9. Trees suitable for the small garden and which will not become too big over the years, will be found in Chapter 7. Underplantings of suitable herbaceous plants and bulbs add greatly to the charm of any shrub garden and a list of suitable subjects will be dealt with in Chapters 16 and 17. Chapter 18 will be devoted to climbers while the final chapters will deal with cultivating, pruning, diseases, and propagation.

Once planted, provided that the beds have first been properly dug and cleaned of all perennial weeds, the small shrub garden needs less maintenance than any other garden form.

The greatest aid to this end is the modern practice of mulching. I shall go into this in more detail in the chapter dealing with soil and cultivation (Chapter 19) but so important is it to the shrub gardener that I feel it necessary to say something about it here.

Most shrubs and trees grow in woodland and in their wild habitat are fed by the heavy annual leaf-fall of other shrubs and trees. In the garden this leaf-fall may be imitated by the spreading of a thick (four- to six-inch) blanket of peat, leaf-mould, chopped bracken, or compost over the surface of the shrub beds so that it not only feeds the shrubs but also helps to prevent the soil drying out and effectively smothers most weeds while any weeds rooting in the mulch material are easily pulled out by hand. I like to supplement the annual autumn mulch by a mulch of green bracken cut and chopped in June. This is of particular benefit to rhododendrons, azaleas, and all lime-hating plants and also to roses, seeming to intensify their colour as well as encouraging healthy growth.

In planning a shrub garden one aims to keep down the costs of labour and upkeep while at the same time achieving the maximum effect of both blossom and restful greenery. To this end it is helpful to keep in mind the following points:

(a) The proportion of flowering evergreens to deciduous shrubs should be high—a ratio of 3 : 2 not being excessive (the under-planting whether shrubby or herbaceous should be mainly evergreen).

(b) Care must be taken to allow for the ultimate spread of trees and shrubs, at the same time remembering that shade-bearing shrubs may be planted to within a few feet of the trunk of standard deciduous trees such as ornamental cherries, crab-apples, etc.

(c) Provision should be made for bloom throughout the year as well as for autumn foliage effect, and winter berries. In the small garden it is best to spread the seasonal effects evenly throughout the garden rather than to restrict sections to shrubs which bloom at any particular time.

(d) When choosing shrubs and underplantings for a small garden due thought should be given to length of flowering-time and effectiveness when out of bloom as well as to individual bloom and garden value when in flower. It is the combination of these four factors which constitutes garden-worthiness.

(e) A small garden has room for only the very best and so it is often necessary tactfully to discard the would-be helpful offerings of friends and neighbours.

(f) Some alpines associate well with shrubs. The use of slate slabs or flat stones as mowing stones to edge a border can offer crevice homes to various thymes, campanulas and dianthus species, while one or two low outcrops sited in bays among low growing shrubs at the forefront of the border will give an opportunity to grow lithospermums, gentians, dwarf pen-stemons, dwarf veronicas, helianthemums, thrift and other suitable subjects.

2

A Formal Shrub Garden

Shrub gardening lends itself admirably to the construction of a small formal garden. There is a wide choice of shrubs with formal lines; and, by the use of dwarf evergreens, the foreground may always be clothed. The spires of columnar growers such as the silvery-blue *Chamaecyparis lawsoniana* 'Fletcheri' (12×5), the pencil-slim grey-foliaged *C. lawsoniana* 'Grayswood Pillar' (15×3) from Italy, and the slender *Juniperus communis* 'Hibernica' (7×2), contrast well, on acid soil, with the mounds of such small-growing rhododendrons as the cherry-crimson 'Elizabeth' ($2\frac{1}{2} \times 4$), the pretty foliaged, pink flowered 'Dormouse' (3×3), 'Bowbells' (3×3), and the yellow 'Cowslip' (3×3). On alkaline soils the evergreen viburnums such as *Viburnum davidii* (3×4) may be used with dwarf genistas, choisya (5×5), and such plants as rosemary (6×5), lavender ($2\frac{1}{2} \times 3$), and the hardier cistuses. These evergreens and evergreys should run through the borders, providing interest and form the year round. The intervening spaces may be filled with flowery deciduous shrubs such as *V. carlesii* (6×6), *Prunus tenella* (3×4)—the dwarf Russian almond—philadelphus, diervilla, Hortensia and lacecap hydrangeas, *P.* 'Amanogawa' (15×3)—the maypole cherry—azaleas, lilacs, the smaller of the longer blooming shrub roses, and the decorative Japanese maples.

Shrub borders may surround a lawn or a paved space with perhaps a formal pool in the middle. Paving looks particularly well in a formal garden. It may be of natural stone or, where expense must be kept down, of cement blocks watered with ferrous sulphate (one pound per gallon of water to treat fifteen square yards in two applications) to give the colour of weather-worn stone. Such paving may be bedded in sand or to save labour it may be set on a cement bed with the joints cemented. Pockets of soil here and there might be left to provide homes for creeping thymes, easy campanulas, bugloss, and alpines tough enough not to mind being trodden on occasionally.

Paving allows the encroachment of shrub growth without the inconvenience caused by attempting to mow where such growth overflows on to the grass. An excellent effect is obtained by planting *Cotoneaster microphyllus* (3 × 6) with its pleasant, small, evergreen foliage where it may spread on to the stones. This cotoneaster has a habit similar to that of the better-known but deciduous *C. horizontalis* (5 × 8). Like *C. horizontalis*, *C. microphyllus* bears attractive berries in winter.

Where the edge is not paved, the front of the border should be curved so that the shrubs may be kept back from the edges without giving too harshly rigid an appearance. Care must be taken to prevent such curves from looking small and niggly. They should follow a bold sweeping line. In the formal garden bulbs should not be planted in the grass. The lawn should present a groomed appearance at all times and the presence of bulbs would prevent mowing until the foliage died down in June. Square flags may be set consecutively in the turf to make a path following the line of the border or, even more effective, such flags should be set level with the turf as formal stepping-stones. Good garden ornaments such as a simple bird-bath, a seat, or a lead figure will give point and add charm to the setting. Or emphasis may be achieved by the careful placing of a specimen tree or shrub.

Even an informal garden may have a formal terrace where house and garden meet. This may be clearly demarked by a line of hydrangeas against a low wall—the lacecaps (3½ × 5) such as *Hydrangea* 'Blue Wave', 'Mariesii' and 'Veitchii' look particularly well in association with masonry, but they need some shade. In sun, the mop-headed Hortensia varieties (5 × 5) will do better. Where there is no wall, the division may be emphasized by a line of evergreens such as choisya, the red-berried *Skimmia japonica* 'Foremanii' (4 × 4)—which is self-fertile and so can be relied upon to produce a good crop of berries each year—or *Viburnum davidii*. This viburnum makes a low, spreading bush with bold, evergreen foliage. An added attraction are the bright turquoise berries which it carries in the autumn. Cross-pollination is necessary to ensure fruiting and so *V. davidii* should be grown in groups. For a terrace twenty-feet long about five bushes would be needed. Always be sure to ask the nurseryman to supply one male form of this viburnum to every group of female bushes.

The corners of a terrace or paved sitting-out place call for special treatment. The winter-flowering *Mahonia japonica* (7×5) is a striking plant for such a position. It has handsome, pinnate, toothed leaves up to a foot in length. Its flowers are bright yellow, carried in long, arching sprays and having a scent of lilies of the valley. In time *M. japonica* will reach six or more feet in height and it is a truly noble plant for an important place in the garden. There used to exist considerable confusion of identity between *M. japonica* and the similar but less desirable *M. bealei*. This has now largely been cleared up, but it is still as well to state when ordering that you require the species with long flower-sprays, the true *M. japonica*, and that no other plant will be acceptable. As an additional check, examine the shrub on arrival. If the terminal leaflet of the pinnate leaves is considerably broader than the others then you have *M. bealei* and not the *M. japonica* you ordered and you should send it back because you will never be satisfied with its stubby, upright spikes of flower and squat leaves when the more elegant *M. japonica* should have been yours. The earlier-blooming hybrid 'Charity' is beautiful, too, with deeper gold cockades.

A shrub rose would be pleasant to fill a corner of the terrace. As a rule for the small garden I would plant only the so-called 'perpetual'-flowering shrub roses which have at least three recurrent seasons of bloom but *Rosa rubrifolia* is an exception. For a cool corner it is unbeatable. Its plum tinted, blue-grey foliage is even more attractive than the single, pink flowers which it complements so well. Throughout the summer it is delightful. It is useful to cut to supply foliage for indoor flower decorations, and towards autumn its leaves take on more glowing tints. To get the greatest beauty from its foliage it should be hard-pruned each year.

A poor, sun-baked border against the south wall of the house is the ideal spot to grow the lavender flowered *Iris unguicularis* (*stylosa*) which is so generous with its blooms from December, or earlier, until March. In addition to the type it is worth growing the white form of this iris. The two are delightful when pulled together for the house. These irises rejoice in drought and poor soil. Any attempt to improve their lot by copious watering or feeding with manure or fertilizers will result in lush growth at the expense of flowers. Slugs are their main enemy and a dressing of 'Slug-it' should be watered round the clumps in December when flower-buds may be expected. Prodigal with its flowers though *I. unguicularis* may be when established, it will often not flower for the first two years, so makers of new gardens should be patient and give it three years' grace before despairing. Provided it has been planted in the conditions described, flowers can positively be guaranteed from the third year on, through the next decade after which the clumps may need dividing and replanting.

The winter jasmine, *Jasminum nudiflorum*, will yield its best show of flowers in such a sunny bed. This jasmine is particularly obliging in its propensity for layering itself where any of its stems touch the ground. Such layers may, of course, be detached and planted in other positions. A wall is not necessary for success and a plant in each aspect, north, south, east, and west will yield the longest possible show of flowers. Underplant your jasmine with the rose and blue forms of the Greek *Anemone blanda*, add the mauve and amethyst chalices of *Crocus tomasinianus* with the subtly shaded varieties of the anemone 'St. Bavo' to follow, and you have a spring border that will give you great pleasure.

Other good plants for a formal terrace are the hypericums—'Hidcote' or 'Rowallane' if your garden is mild—*Hypericum forrestii* if it is more exposed. Their golden, bowl-shaped flowers show particularly well against stone.

A good herbaceous perennial to associate with paving or walls is the Corsican hellebore—*Helleborus argutifolius* (*corsicus*)—with boldly sculptured, holly-toothed leaves and clusters of nodding, bowl-shaped flower-heads in chartreuse-green.

An aspect of formal gardening which very much appeals to me

is the construction of a series of small garden enclosures within the garden, each surrounded by its own hedge and forming a complete unity. These small enclosures may be attractively furnished by shrubs together with lilies, paeonies, and herbaceous plants with distinctive foliage such as bergenias (megasea), hostas (funkias), acanthus, *Cyclamen neapolitanum*, etc.

Although the classic examples of such gardens are on the grand scale as at Hidcote Manor in Gloucestershire and Tintinhull House in Somerset, the idea may be used with equally good effect in a small, modern garden. A long, narrow, back garden might be divided into three portions. The first might be paved and have a shade tree in the corner with bushes of rosemary or clipped holly and clumps of thyme in the paving and borders of mop-head hydrangeas, mock oranges, mahonia, and hypericum, fronted by hostas and bergenias and backed by a thuja hedge.

Through a gap in a lavender hedge, steps or perhaps a wrought-iron gate might lead into a second garden. This garden should, to change the emphasis, have a pool or sundial in the middle. On acid soil its borders might be planted with evergreen azaleas, a spreading juniper, and dwarf rhododendrons, with lilies interplanted. On limy soil, hybrid musk roses might take the place of the rhododendrons and azaleas. The third garden might have apple or ornamental cherry trees in grass underplanted with daffodils, bluebells, camassias, and autumn-flowering colchicums. Beech or hornbeam hedging would provide a suitable background.

A corner site offers itself admirably to the arrangement of separate garden units. The front garden would present one unity, perhaps with a pool as central theme, edged by foliage borders with blue and gold foliaged shrubs and coloured maples. The side garden might consist of a lawn running between curved azalea and lily borders and leading into a third garden at the back which might contain an outcrop of rock to one side with heaths over-swept by a Japanese maple and edged by dwarf evergreen shrubs enclosing a miniature lawn.

Suitable shrubs for the blue and gold garden would be the blue *Chamaecyparis lawsoniana* 'Chilworth Silver' (8×8); *C.* 'Fletcheri' and *C. pisifera* 'Boulevard' (12×8); the spreading *Juniperus squamata* 'Meyeri' (6×8) with the golden, dwarf, spreading *Hebe armstrongii*; golden privet; *Chamaecyparis lawsoniana* 'Winston Churchill' (15×8); the thuja 'Rheingold' (4×2); golden variegated hollies, the golden foliaged heath—*Calluna* 'Gold Haze'; the cut-leaved golden elder—*Alnus incana* 'Laciniata'; *Cornus alba* 'Spaethii' (7×6)—a dogwood with golden marginal foliage; golden box, and *Elaeagnus pungens* 'Maculata' (6×6).

Purple-leafed maples such as *Acer palmatum* 'Atropurpureum' (7×5) and *A. p.* 'Dissectum Atropurpureum' (3×3) would make a bold contrast and would look particularly well above the bluish foliage of the spreading juniper, with a blue cypress in the background.

Japanese garden design has made its influence felt on the Western world. One useful concept of this for the small garden, which has reached us via New Zealand, is the Pebble Garden. A formal adaptation of this might consist of curved beds flowing round a central swathe of grass to represent a river. The beds, carefully prepared to incorporate moist peat and rotted compost, are mulched with heavy grade black polythene. Crosses are cut in the polythene through which are planted shrubs of striking form (dwarf conifers, Japanese maples, chaeonomeles, evergreen azaleas, mahonias and the like) and the surface is covered with pebbles of attractive shape and colouring, representing the banks of the 'river' upon which the vegetation is growing. A little charcoal incorporated with the peat helps to keep the soil sweet under the polythene.

3

Shrubs for the Small Formal Border

Heaths, both winter- and summer-flowering, are among the best evergreen carpeters for the front of a formal shrub border. While the summer-flowering species will thrive only on acid soil, the winter-blooming *Erica carnea* ($\frac{3}{4} \times 1\frac{1}{2}$), its varieties, and the hybrid *E. × darleyensis* ($1\frac{1}{2} \times 2$) do not object to lime. A handful of peat or leaf-mould around the roots at planting-time helps them to become established, and if peat or rotted bracken is incorporated in the bed and sand is added in very heavy soils, they will grow in almost any garden.

The *E. carnea* varieties form spreading mats about nine inches high. The first to flower in November is the dwarf, crimson-pink 'Eileen Porter' ($\frac{1}{2} \times \frac{3}{4}$); 'Winter Beauty'—a pleasant bright pink— follows in December to be joined by 'King George'—rosy-crimson —in January. *E. c.* 'Praecox', a warm flesh-pink, and the deeper 'James Backhouse' are the next to bloom along with 'Springwood', an incomparable, widely spreading white variety with striking tan coloured anthers which protrude from the mouth of the bells. In late February and March, 'Ruby Glow' and the deep red 'Vivelli' with its bronzy, dark foliage complete the season. A mixed drift of winter heaths makes a flowery and delightful picture. With the exception of 'Springwood', the *E. carnea* varieties should be planted at a distance of a foot apart. 'Springwood' should be given at least eighteen inches from plant to plant. Like the others it is easily increased by mound-layering. In autumn a mixture of peat and leaf-mould should be applied as a mulch and worked into the plants so that only the tops of the branches protrude. By the following autumn the individual stems will have formed roots and be ready to detach from the parent to form a new bed.

E. × darleyensis is more straggling in growth and so less useful in the small, formal garden. In less formal places it makes a bushy plant with trailing spikes of pale pink flowers that appear sporadically from November on. In our garden its best effect in cold winters is sometimes delayed until March. The deeper pink *E. × darleyensis* 'Arthur Johnson' blooms earlier and is a better plant. Also good is the white *E. mediterranea* 'W.T. Rackliff' (2×3). This makes a vigorous but compact bush which flowers in February and March. It has fresh green foliage against which the white bells are particularly delightful, and is useful to give height to drifts of the lower growing *E. carnea* varieties.

Beware of planting the deeper coloured 'Ruby Glow' and 'Vivelli' next to the whites, the colour change is too extreme. 'Springwood' should merge into a drift of pink such as 'James Backhouse' or 'Springwood Pink' which in turn may mingle with the brighter colours.

These heaths look best in irregular drifts composed of one variety with adjacent varieties overlapping slightly. Like all heaths they should be clipped over after flowering to keep their growth compact. Neglect of this will eventually result in straggly bushes which become bare at the centre. Where this has happened the plants should be pruned hard back into the old wood. Heaths break readily from old wood and such treatment usually ensures plenty of fresh, vigorous growth.

For acid or neutral soils the Cornish heath, *E. vagans* ($1\frac{1}{2} \times 3$) in its varieties 'Mrs. Maxwell' (deep rose) and 'Lyonesse' (white) is among the best summer-flowering heaths. The Cornish heath makes three-foot-wide mounds of bottle-brush spikes and in winter its close, dark foliage is distinctive. It is a vigorous grower and each plant should be allowed a space at least two feet square.

To give later colour, varieties of the common ling—*Calluna vulgaris* (2×2)—are useful and effective. 'H.E. Beale' is a vigorous double-flowered lilac variety with long and showy spikes of bloom while 'J.H. Hamilton' is dwarfer with double pink flowers that remind one of tiny *centifolia* roses. *C. vulgaris* 'Hammondii' ($2\frac{1}{2} \times 2$) is to my mind the best single white. *C. v.* 'Alba Plena' ($1\frac{1}{2} \times 2$) is a pleasing and showy white, double-flowered variety. *C. v.* 'Alportii' and 'Goldsworth Crimson' (2×2) are good late-flowering reds. *Erica tetralix*, the cross-leaved heath, is pretty, especially in its varieties 'Rosea' and 'Praegerae' and in *t.* 'Alba Mollis', a superb white with foliage of frosty looking greyish green. These heaths prefer a moist soil, as does the pretty Dorset heath, *E. ciliaris* (1×2). In our garden *E. cinerea* ($1 \times 1\frac{1}{2}$), the native bell-heather, is more difficult. It needs a sandy, moorland soil and full exposure to do really well. The varieties *E. c.* 'Coccinea', *E. c.* 'C.D. Eason' and *E. c.* 'Atrosanguinea' are particularly good.

Daboecia (2×3) is a close ally of the ericas. The Irish heath has large egg-shaped bells, sometimes purple, sometimes white and in one variety bi-coloured. All forms of this heath are desirable, but the white *D. alba* with its pristine globules is the most showy and attractive of all.

For gardens on acid or neutral soils, dwarf evergreen azaleas are excellent first-row plants. Always neat and trim with foliage which in some varieties turns red and crimson for the winter and which in others remains a fresh, contrasting green, they are decorative the year round. Some of the later-flowering varieties need dappled shade to prevent the too-rapid fading of their flowers, and all should be given a shovelful of moist peat round the root-ball at planting. This is particularly helpful with plants imported from Holland which have usually been grown in pure black peat and find it difficult to adapt themselves to ordinary garden soil. Peat placed around the roots and mixed with the surrounding soil helps to make the adjustment easier and encourages the roots to spread. Evergreen azaleas are much less sensitive to alkalinity than are many members of the rhododendron genus. I have had them thriving for years in a decidedly alkaline soil with which rotted bracken and peat has been incorporated, and to which a mulch of chopped green bracken is added each summer.

By choosing successive varieties it is possible to have evergreen azaleas in flower from April to June. They look well planted in groups of four to six plants, merging on either side into heaths, candytuft, rock roses (helianthemums), or similar dwarf evergreens.

Some of these small azaleas will eventually become sizeable bushes reaching a height of three feet with a four or five foot spread. They are, however, highly portable, so one may plant them close enough for immediate effect and, as they grow, move every other plant to a different part of the garden to start a new grouping.

'Kirin' is usually the first to flower and within a few days of the opening of its rose-pink, hose-in-hose bells, 'Hinodegiri' and 'Hatsugiri'—in crimson and purple respectively—come into bloom. Probably the best known of all is 'Hinomayo' which flowers perhaps a week later and has wide-open, phlox-pink flowers and bright apple-green foliage. These four associate charmingly together. Their colours are bright, clean and yet not garish, but they must be kept away from orange and vermilion varieties. The purple of 'Hatsugiri' should be separated from the crimson 'Hinodegiri' by one or other of the pink varieties.

'Hinodegiri' has enough scarlet in its make-up to look well with the oranges and flames and so can be used in a second group with 'Orange Beauty' ('Hinodegiri' × *kaempferi*) or 'Sakata'. It is past its best by the time 'John Cairns' begins to flower. 'John Cairns' belongs to the larger-flowered and often taller-growing group of *malvatica* × *kaempferi* hybrids. Many of these have strong flower colours which are apt to fade in direct sunlight, so a shady spot should be chosen for them. They have a distinctive and attractive tiered habit of growth, something like that of a miniature cedar of Lebanon. Among the prettiest are 'Feodora' (rose-pink), 'Addy Wery' (vermilion with very good foliage), 'Willy' (orange), 'Garden Beauty' (soft pink), 'Jeanette' (rosy-red), 'Atalanta' (lilac), 'Palestrina' (white), and the brilliant but tender 'Bengal Fire' which is in fact *kaempferi* × *oldhamii*.

These hybrids look well in groups of three contrasting or complementary colours. Some gardeners prefer a Russian ballet group of all the colours with white to intervene between the more violently opposed shades. I think the whites are charming grouped with the pink and lavender hybrids but prefer to keep them away from the stronger colours. Many of them are effective as solitary plants but on the whole I think they look better grouped. To extend the dwarf azalea season, the May-June flowering 'Gumpos' may be added with their frilly semi-double flowers in white or shades of pink. These are delightful little azaleas which should find a place in every formal shrub garden. Recently the useful June-flowering, Ferndown hybrids have been added. These were raised by Messrs. Stewarts' Nurseries at Ferndown in Dorset and include such attractive plants as the dwarf, large-flowered, deep pink 'Vida Brown'; 'Clarissa' in pale salmon-orange with frilly, hose-in-hose flowers; 'Cerita', a stronger growing azalea with mandarin-red flowers; 'Lady Elphinstone', salmon-pink, and the blood-red 'Martin Stewart'. There is also the June-blooming *Azalea kaempferi* 'Mikado'.

A simple formal border might consist of these evergreen azaleas, edged by a front row of *Erica carnea* varieties, with lacecap or Hortensia hydrangeas behind, backed by the tall, summer-flowering Mount Etna broom *Genista aetnensis* (8×6).

For a shady border the lacecap hydrangeas are to my mind the most telling with their interesting heads of bead-like, fertile flowers surrounded by large showy sterile florets, often in a different shade. Where strong colour is wanted and the soil is free from lime, 'Blue Wave' is the variety to choose with both ray and disk florets in a clear, bright blue. More subtle effects may be obtained from *Hydrangea* 'Mariesii' with blue inner flowers and lilac outer, *H.* 'Veitchii' whose fertile flowers are turquoise surrounded by large white sterile florets, 'Blue Bird', with flower-heads in two delicate but brilliant shades of blue, and the five-foot high 'Grayswood' whose white sterile florets turn to deep red as the flowers age. On alkaline soils 'Blue Wave', 'Blue Bird' and *H.* 'Mariesii' will have lilac to pink flowers while the fertile florets of *H.* 'Veitchii' and 'Grayswood' will probably be pink.

Genista aetnensis should be staked and trained to single or double stem so that its firefly flowers shower over the hydrangeas in golden veils. To complete the scheme one may use yellow or amber roses such as *Rosa rugosa* 'Agnes' or the hybrid musk rose 'Grandmaster', a rose which is often said to be a poor 'doer' but which is so valuable for the uncommon amber of its cupped, semi-double blooms that it is worth trouble to get it to succeed. Hard pruning, mulching with green bracken in June, and feeding with Murphy Sequestrene is the recipe for success. With the yellow roses one might plant the pink rugosa 'Sarah van Fleet'. On limy soils the hydrangea flowers will be pink and there the crimson-purple 'Roseraie de l'Hay', and the white 'Blanc double de Coubert' will be the most effective.

A border consisting of a double row of a dozen evergreen azaleas, five lacecap hydrangeas, and four rugosa roses interspersed by three Mount Etna brooms would need to be thirty feet long by at least ten feet wide. The planting should be staggered, with the plants in each successive row filling the gap between the plants in the row in front.

To supplement the winter-flowering heaths, which do well in almost any soil, in districts where the ground is on the acid side of neutral there are now several good cultivars of calluna (ling) with coloured foliage. These look well at the forefront of a formal border.

Chief among the newer callunas that are good in flower as well as foliage are: 'Fred J. Chapple', with spring foliage in shades of greeny gold, pink and copper followed by prolific purple flowers; 'Gold Haze', which keeps its brilliant gold foliage throughout the year and bears long white flower sprays; 'Multicolor' ('Prairie Fire'), with yellow-green foliage, the tips of which burn to red in winter, followed by bronze young growth and pale purple blooms, and 'Robert Chapman', with golden-bronze foliage becoming fiery in winter and carrying good flower sprays in late August and September.

4

Plants for the Larger Border

Many small houses have long, narrow gardens at the rear, while often a small detached house has a stretch of garden at the side, joining the front and back plots. This gives scope for a more extensive, formal shrub border.

Such a border should be at least ten feet wide—more where space allows. It may either be edged with paving stone so as to allow shrubs to grow forward to break a too-harsh outline, or it may follow a sweeping curve and perhaps take in the far boundary of the garden.

Here, as in the smaller border, thought should be given to evergreen plantings to give form to the whole and to ensure a neat and orderly appearance. Deciduous shrubs and small trees may be included, but the main structure and the foreground of the border should consist of evergreen flowering shrubs and perennials to make a close 'boskage' to keep down weeds.

'Boskage' is an old word originally used to denote a close ground covering of shrubs with woodland flowers between and now used by many gardeners to describe such a community of lowly shrubs and evergreen perennials densely covering the ground. I am told that African pygmies have fifty-three words for 'forest' in their very limited vocabulary, because they need to convey its thickness, sorts of trees, undergrowth, and likely game. Gardeners hitherto had nothing between 'canopy' used more by foresters for when trees crowd into a shade, and 'carpet' for ground cover. So, needing one for shrubs with the foliage meeting solidly enough not to need weeding, not unnaturally they brought back 'boskage' from the 'grene wode'-covered England when a bosky dell meant one with thickets of shrubs round it and woodland flowers between—just like our garden.

Interesting evergreen perennials to help make up such a boskage might include the leathery-leafed bergenias, periwinkles, and hellebores together with the helianthemums and dwarf brooms such as early creamy *Cytisus* × *kewensis* (1 × 4), the later, golden flowered *Genista lydia* (1 × 3), and the double Dyer's greenweed —*G. tinctoria* 'Plena' ($\frac{1}{2}$ × 2)—to give variety to the plantings of heaths and dwarf azaleas. On limy soils the azaleas would have to give way to candytuft and *Erica carnea* or, in mild coastal areas, to the bright blue, evergreen *Aster pappei*. This is hardy enough to stand mild winters with us on the coast of North Wales, but inland it would have to be lifted or given winter protection. It associates well with yellow or orange helianthemums.

The best of the helianthemums are particularly useful for foreground cover as their evergreen foliage forms dense mats six inches thick, successfully suppressing any weed seedlings. Strong-growing upright varieties must be chosen, planted nine inches apart, and closely clipped in July, after the first flush of flower is over, so that they give a second burst of bloom in September and build up a dense foliage cover before the winter.

Some helianthemums are straggly growers but 'Ben Dearg' (soft red), 'Ben Fhada' (yellow), 'Ben More' (orange), 'Rhodanthe Carneum' (soft pink), 'Taylor's Seedling' (orange-scarlet) and 'Wisley Primrose' are all vigorous, upright-growing varieties that are particularly suitable for the task. They may be planted either in mixed drifts when they will give a gay, but perhaps restless, kaleidoscopic effect, or—and this to my mind is the best way— in drifts and bays of separate colours.

After about seven or eight years the plants may become straggly and should be renewed from two-inch cuttings taken with a heel in August and rooted in sand and peat under glass (either a bell-jar or sunny window-sill will suffice). They must be kept moist until rooted. It is safest to winter the cuttings indoors and plant them out in nursery rows the following spring when they will quickly make sturdy young bushes for transplanting to their final quarters in the autumn.

In a border such as we have in mind, one might bring to the front the interesting cut-leaf, dwarf maple *Acer palmatum* 'Dissectum'. Nearby a fastigiate grower such as *Chamaecyparis l.* 'Ellwoodii' or the upright cherry *Prunus* 'Amanogawa' (syn. *P. serrulata erecta*) would give contrast and emphasis.

There are several colour forms of the cut-leaf maple. *Acer palmatum* 'Dissectum Atropurpureum' would make a good combination with the glaucous *Chamaecyparis l.* 'Ellwoodii' or *C. l.* 'Fletcheri'. The type with its fresh green, slightly bronze tinted foliage is also a fine plant. Both form slow-growing, mushroom-like shrubs, more compact in habit than the scap-leafed maple, *Acer palmatum* 'Atropurpureum' which also is slow growing enough to be put to a similar use. All shrubs used for their distinctive foliage should be placed towards the front of the border. The purple-leafed maples are particularly effective planted where the rays of the sinking sun will shine through the foliage.

On acid soil, medium-growing evergreens to give summer colour and winter form to the border might include the more compact rhododendrons. 'Britannia' (5×7) is a low-growing hardy hybrid with crimson flowers in early June. 'Goldfinch' (7×7) is earlier and bears pink flowers which are yellow in the throat, while 'Blue Peter' (7×7) is an attractive lavender. All these are suitable for colder gardens. For more favoured gardens in the South and near the west coast—or anywhere in Britain where reasonably sheltered conditions prevail (with some shade in the South and East) one might choose the attractive first-cross hybrids —'Fabia' (5×5) with orange-scarlet flowers; the bright red 'May Day' (5×5); 'Lady Chamberlain' (4×3) with lapageria-like bells in orange-salmon and pretty bluish foliage and its lovely pink counterpart 'Lady Rosebery'; the bright yellow 'Marcia' (5×5); waxy, terracotta-scarlet 'Romany Chal' (4×6); daffodil 'Jalisco' (5×5); the deep pink 'Flashlight' (5×5), or the early, milk-white 'Carex' (5×5), delicately spotted with chocolate at the throat.

Shade for these rhododendrons can be provided by a flowering cherry or crab-apple planted to their south. *Prunus serrulata longipes*, also known as 'Shimidsu', ('Oku Miyako') (12×8) is an effective, moderate-growing cherry for the small garden with its long-stalked (hence *longipes*), fimbriated, white flowers that are as frilly and as pretty as the *tutu* of a ballet dancer. It is one of the last cherries to flower and will often coincide with the hardy, blue rhododendron 'Susan' (6×7) to create a pleasant border picture.

In our garden we have a semi-double cherry called 'Oshukun' (15×8) with blooms of a gentle malmaison-pink. This is earlier to flower than 'Shimidsu' and is decorative with its beautifully shaped flowers that seem more freely borne than those of any other cherry. In autumn its colouring is among the best of all the cherries, its leaves turning to shades of strawberry and crimson that rival even the Liquidamber. Unfortunately 'Oshukun' is no longer very easy to obtain although I think some of the bigger nurseries would be able to supply it were they asked.

Most gardeners like to have a lilac (12×10) in their garden, and there are so many good varieties available that choice is merely a matter of personal taste. Two which I would recommend are 'Prodige' with enormous flowers of purple-lavender (each floret being an inch across) and 'Sensation' with purple-red flowers edged with white and carried in large trusses to give a chintzy and delightful effect. The true pink *Syringa × josiflexa* 'Bellicent', although less fragrant, also gives us much pleasure. You will usually find lilacs listed under the generic name *Syringa*.

Most of the equally popular philadelphus, or mock oranges, are too big for a modest border. Two which are suitable are 'Bouquet Blanc' (a pretty double which may grow to a height of five or six feet but seldom occupies more than a yard square and is good for the middle or back of the border) and 'Manteau d'Hermine' which should be planted towards the front, being more low and spreading than 'Bouquet Blanc'. It has creamy-white double flowers. I would plant both varieties to balance each other.

An effective plant to use with advantage towards the front of a formal border is *Viburnum plicatum* 'Mariesii' with flowers that remind one of the lacecap hydrangeas with an inner disk of bead-like, fertile flowers and showy sterile outer blooms. The flower-head is white. These striking blooms contrast with velvety green leaves

carried on flat, horizontal-growing branches and the whole plant
has great architectural quality. Less compelling in form, but
valuable for its scented flowers in spring, is *V. carlesii* with bun-
shaped heads of tubular florets which are rosy in bud but open to
waxen whiteness. The pink buds give a rosy flush to the whole
flower-head so that the colour effect is similar to that of apple-
blossom with the advantage of a haunting, jasmine-like fragrance.
At the front of the border, preferably near a path where one
might bend to pluck it in winter, another viburnum—*V. farreri*
'Nanum' (1×2)—might be grown. This viburnum bears small
pinky-white heads of flower, with a sweet hawthorn scent, from
November to spring. Some people say that *V. farreri* 'Nanum'
does not flower freely but the established bushes I know flower even
more freely than the bigger type, though they may take a long
time to reach this stage. Like the type they need a sunny, open
position to give their best. They sucker freely so if the thicket
seems overcrowded, shoots may be detached to form new bushes.

For the front of the border, evergreen daphnes such as *Daphne
collina neapolitana* ($\frac{1}{2} \times 1$) and the winter-blooming *D. × hybrida* are
attractive. On limy soil they may be used to replace the ever-
green rhododendrons and azaleas along with the red berried
Skimmia japonica 'Foremanii' and a group of the turquoise fruited
Viburnum davidii. In such gardens the missing spring brilliance of
rhododendrons and azaleas may be supplied by ornamental quinces
such as *Chaenomeles* 'Knap Hill Scarlet' (5×6) and *C.* 'Simonii'
(3×6) and the terracotta 'Boule de Feu' (5×6). Where the presence
of lime is not overwhelming, coloured hybrid brooms (*Cytisus*)
(6×5) will do well. They should be kept compact by shearing
immediately flowering is over, otherwise they become subject to
wind-rock and will not live so long. *Cytisus × praecox* (4×4) and
the genistas do not seem to object to any amount of alkalinity.

Shrub roses should find a place in every border. For a small
formal border the hybrid musks (5×6)—'Felicia' (pink), 'Penelope'
(paler pink), 'Bonn' (crimson), 'Moonlight' (white), and 'Buff
Beauty'—would be the most appropriate. They should not be
pruned too much and should be allowed to make large, natural-
shaped bushes.

One of the best small trees to plant as a specimen at the edge of paving, or on a lawn, or at the side of a border to give height is the weeping rosebud cherry, *Prunus subhirtella* 'Pendula Rosea' (6 × 6). This is not a very vigorous grower and should not be exposed to wind. Grown on a short leg it is very pretty with its trailing branches showered with rosy flowers in April. Where this might be caught by frost one could substitute the later blooming, rosette-flowered *P.* 'Kiku-shidare Sakura' (8 × 6), sometimes wrongly referred to as 'Cheal's Weeping Cherry'. The occasional pinching out of the trailing tips of the branches of this variety in summer will ensure plenty of side-shoots and flowers for another year.

Of all evergreens, camellias (averaging five foot by four foot after ten years) are among the loveliest for a formal garden. Their glossy foliage alone gives them distinction and their blooms are numerous and carried over a long period in spring. The new hybrid *Camellia* × *williamsii* class gives us some of the finest of all camellias. Camellias of this type are exceptionally early and free with their flowers and have the advantage of blooming freely even in Scotland where *C. japonica* seldom flowers, needing a longer period of daylight than is found in winter in more northern latitudes. The *C.* × *williamsii* hybrids flower earlier than the *C. japonica* hybrids—in February and March—while, following the exceptionally hot summer of 1959 some were in flower at Bodnant in North Wales in November. This habit of early flowering means that they should be given a sheltered situation. Planted against a north or west wall their blooms will often miss the frost; or they might be sited under the spreading branches of a deciduous tree or to the north of a large evergreen. In this way the flowers often escape the damage which would be inevitable in the open garden. With camellias there is always a consolation for frost damage in the fact that the blooms open successively and so there are usually plenty of buds to replace frosted flowers. All camellias, however, should be planted where there is shelter from battering winds.

C. × *w.* 'Donation' is one of the most pleasing of the new hybrids and is reckoned by many to be the finest of all camellias. It has perfectly shaped, semi-double flowers of warm pink, veined in a deeper colour. They open almost to a reflex shape at first and then become slightly trumpet-shaped, lasting for a fortnight in open weather. C.×w. 'Mary Christian' is a special favourite of mine with more trumpet-shaped single blooms in deep phlox-pink borne on a handsome upright bush. Then there is the superb semi-double C.×w. 'Citation' with shapely, pale pink blooms. C.×w. 'J.C. Williams' is a single-flowered variety with paler but attractive flowers of a dog-rose pink. The blooms are three to four inches across and very freely carried. These hybrids have the advantage that they drop their faded blooms instead of letting them remain to disfigure the bush. C.×w. 'St. Ewe' is another good one—this time a deep pink—to watch for when it becomes widely available, while the single, pale pink, Bodnant-raised C.×w. 'Hiraethlyn' is to my mind one of the most delectable of all.

The C. japonica varieties are still the most commonly seen and, south of the Scottish border, give very satisfactory results. Their foliage is dark and shining—more handsome even than that of the C.×williamsii class, and they bear a succession of exotic-looking blooms in early spring, later than many of the C.×williamsii cultivars and so more valuable in cold districts. C. japonica, it is rightly said, is as hardy as laurel, yet the blooms of some varieties are easily spoiled by wind and rain.

The lovely pink C. j. 'Lady Clare' is a favourite in our garden. With its sprawling habit it is an effective plant for the front of the border where it can spread itself over the edge of paving, or for terrace pots in a formal area. Yet its flowers are easily spoiled by weather and for bleaker districts this variety should be replaced by the tougher C. j. 'Gloire de Nantes' with similar, but smaller, rose-pink flowers with a central mass of golden stamens. Early and generous with its blooms, I would place 'Gloire de Nantes' high in the list of reliable varieties for any district and in fact Mr. Puddle tells me that it is the hardiest in flower of all camellias grown in this country. With it one might plant the semi-double C. j. 'Adolphe Audusson'—a very free-flowering variety with particularly pleasing geranium-lake, gold centred blooms and a sturdy upright habit. With us, 'Adolphe Audusson' has proved an exceptionally quick grower, rapidly outstripping 'Lady Clare' and even the vigorous $C. \times w.$ 'Donation', which were planted at the same time.

There seem to be more good semi-double camellias in red than in any other colour. $C. j.$ 'Mercury', $C. j.$ 'Mars'; and the exceptionally hardy, rose-crimson $C. j.$ 'Latifolia' which makes a wide spreading bush are all first-rate garden plants for any district. $C. j.$ 'Magnoliiflora' is another which might be added for the distinction of its form and the gentle prettiness of its soft shell-pink flowers.

Coming to the more formal doubles, $C. j.$ 'C.M. Hovey' is an attractive plant and is one of the most reliable for general outdoor cultivation in England and Wales. $C. j.$ 'Rubescens Major' is another hardy and extremely handsome double red in which the regularly arranged petals are deeply veined in a darker colour. $C. j.$ 'Mathotiana Rosea' is a reasonably weather-proof formal pink and here it must be stated that this variety has no connexion with the confusingly named double red, $C. j.$ 'Mathotiana', which though beautiful is quite useless for outdoor cultivation in most parts of the British Isles, its petals browning dismally at the first puff of wind or splash of rain.

White camellias need the protection of a sheltering evergreen when grown out of doors but given such a luxury, to prevent the rain splashing and browning its petals, $C. j.$ 'Alba Plena' is a formal, white double which will do well in most districts—while for those who, like myself, prefer informal blooms the single $C. j.$ 'Alba Simplex' with its golden centred blooms holds a deserved place as the favourite white variety.

Midway between the singles and semi-doubles (which have more petals but still show the central boss of stamens) come the anemone-flowered camellias in which some of the stamens have become petaloid, and in which the centre is a mixed mass of these petaloids and stamens surrounded by one or more rows of large outer petals giving a flat-shaped bloom. A further development is the paeony form in which the flower is deeper and more rounded with several rows of outer petals surrounding a convex mass of twisted petaloids and stamens. $C. j.$ 'Elegans' is an example of the anemone-flowered type, with pink flowers that are not easily spoiled by wind and rain. Of the paeony-flowered varieties $C. j.$

'Althiiflora' is one of the most weather-resistant. Also good are the red C. j. 'Arejeshi' with deeply cut, coarse but striking foliage and C. j. 'Preston Rose'.

For really cold gardens either the semi-double C. j. 'Latifolia' or the single red C. j. 'Jupiter' are the varieties to choose. Two pink singles which I think very beautiful with their simple form and great bosses of stamens are the rosy C. j. 'Hatsu-sakura' and the paler C. j. 'Apple Blossom' which may be listed in some catalogues as C. j. 'Joy Sanders'.

Quite in place in a formal garden, though not to my mind so suitable for informal plantings, are the striped and variegated varieties. The semi-double C. j. 'Donckelarii' has flowers in which the deep red ground colour is handsomely marbled with white, while the double C. j. 'Tricolor' often bears three different types of bloom on the same bush, some blush flaked with rose and carmine, some pale blush to almost white, and some in deep rose-carmine. C. j. 'Comtesse Lavinia Maggi' is another striped variety which in the right setting has the appeal of the old striped roses beloved by the Dutch flower painters.

For mild districts the November to December flowering sasanqua camellias are delightful. Their foliage is smaller and of a fresher green than the C. japonica varieties and they bear mostly single or semi-double flowers which are not so large as those of the C. japonica varieties and are of a charming and less formal shape. To ensure their flowering freely they need to be planted against a south wall or with their back to an evergreen hedge. As they flower before Christmas the rule about planting where the flowers are shaded from the morning sun does not apply. More important is summer sunshine. Whereas other camellias, particularly C. japonica and its cultivars need shade: the C. sasanqua varieties need sun to ripen the wood and to ensure the production of flower-buds. It is neglect of this that leads to their failure to flower freely in some gardens. Even so, some varieties are not as free-flowering as others. The well-tried C. s. 'Narumi-gata' which was erroneously called C. s. oleifera in many gardens, is reliable with its three-inch, white, pink-tinted, scented, apple-blossom-like flowers which are a great asset to floral decorations in November. C. s. 'Hiryu' flowers in December and January and bears bright rose-carmine, semi-double flowers. *C. s.* 'Crimson King' also blooms at this time and, like 'Hiryu', may be relied upon to flower well in most gardens. Like the rhododendrons, pernettyas, kalmias, and many other desirable evergreens, camellias should be planted in lime-free soil which is rich in humus. To supply the humus, quantities of organic matter in the form of peat, leaf-mould, and rotted cow-manure (if you can get it) mixed with straw should be dug into the top spit. The bottom spit of soil should be broken up; but as the camellia, like the rhododendron, is shallow rooting it is not necessary to enrich the soil below the top spit.

If your soil is alkaline and you have set your heart on growing camellias, do not despair. You may grow them either in tubs (watered with rainwater in case the tap-water contains lime) or, as I have done for years, in the actual garden by digging out holes three feet square and deep, preferably lining them with heavy black polythene provided with drainage holes, and replacing the alkaline soil with lime-free compost. Treatment thereafter with Murphy Sequestrene (which contains iron in a form that can readily be absorbed by the plant along with aluminium, magnesium, and manganese) and mulching with green bracken in June should ensure success. Camellias are in fact less subject to deficiencies caused by lime in the soil than are rhododendrons, and for the gardener on alkaline soil who is prepared to take trouble to grow them well they are therefore a reasonable proposition.

Just as camellias will not grow in alkaline soil without special preparation neither will they grow in extremely acid soil without extra nourishment in the form of annual mulches of rotted cow-manure, watered well in.

In neutral soils and soils where the acidity is slight camellias will do better if mulched annually with chopped bracken in June. When planting camellias in such soils I like to incorporate the top-soil scraped from a bracken bed along with peat in the planting-holes.

Camellias dislike bad drainage and when planting in clay soils it has been found advisable to drain the planting area. In such soils bigger-than-usual planting holes should be dug in early autumn and left open through the winter. Wind and frost will work the soil so that in spring it will be found possible to break down the clay and to incorporate peat and rotten bracken. Clay soils should always be worked in dry weather as wet weather makes them so sticky that it is impossible to break down the lumps.

Although they need good drainage camellias also need a certain amount of moisture and so they should never be planted where the soil is likely to dry out completely.

Established camellias should be fed with a light mulch of rotted cow-manure, watered well in during the spring when the bushes are making new growth. Murphy Sequestrene is a valuable feed for camellias as well as for azaleas, roses, and hydrangeas.

Apart from the chlorosis of the leaves, shown by yellowing, in plants suffering from alkaline poisoning, the ailments of camellias are fortunately rare. There is a virus which causes a mottled yellowing of the leaves and may also cause some variegation in the bloom but it does not seem to do any real harm and there is no known cure for the condition although good cultivation will camouflage the trouble by reducing the blotching. Applications of soot-water, urea, well-rotted cow-manure, and watering with Murphy Sequestrene dissolved in water are usually efficacious in reducing the symptoms. Given suitable soil conditions and reasonable wind-shelter camellias are among the easiest and most rewarding of evergreen flowering shrubs.

5

Less Formal Plantings

If shrubs may be happily used to make a formal garden they are to me at any rate, even more delightful in an informal scheme where one has more scope for varying effects obtained by using shrubs of freer growth with a wider choice of underplanting.

Satisfying colour pictures may be built up by the complementary association of shrubs and carpeters which flower at the same time. *Hamamelis mollis* (7×7), though lovely on its own when its golden tinsel flowers star its bare branches, is even more effective when underplanted with a carpet of *Erica carnea* 'Winter Beauty' and given the company of the rose-purple, butterfly flowers of *Rhododendron mucronulatum* (5×5), the scented blooms of the purple-red *Daphne mezereum* (2×3), and the maroon bowls of *Helleborus atrorubens* near by. These may share the same carpeting of winter heath or it may be varied by underplantings of *Primula juliae* or even 'Wanda' which loses its banality in such company, particularly when the cold blues its magenta flowers to a more comely violet. Blue primroses may be interplanted with the 'Wanda' to good effect.

Magnolia stellata (4×3) is another beauty of the early months of the year, making a twiggy bush of strikingly Japanese aspect, seldom more than ten feet in height and less through, even when fully grown. The irregular, yet pleasing outline of its rather floppy flowers finds expression in the *stellata* ('star-like') of its specific name, and the solid whiteness of its petals can best be set off by underplanting a sheet of muscari beneath its boughs so that it sails like a tea-clipper on a sea of blue.

Often, it is argued, such colour effects do not come off. The timing of one plant may be advanced by the season and that of the other retarded. Admittedly this is sometimes the case, although I have never known the timing of *M. stellata* and the *Muscari* 'Heavenly Blue' not to coincide. Yet even if the effect were to succeed in only three years out of five, would it not more than justify the small amount of planning involved?

Flowering cherries are such big guns in the spring campaign that their blossom against the sky is often reckoned of sufficient beauty in itself. Even the most modest garden, however, has room to complement the effect of its single cherry or group of cherries by a fitting underplanting. The 'Amanogawa' (15×3) or 'Mikuruma-gaeshi' (15×8) will look even lovelier if their soft pink blossoms are spread above the rhododendron 'Blue Tit' ($2\frac{1}{2} \times 3$), while 'Blue Tit's' harebell-blue flowers will take on greater clarity by the juxtaposition of the creamy-yellow, dwarf broom *Cytisus × kewensis*. On limed soils a similar colour picture could be obtained by using the blue *Omphalodes verna* while the deeper *O. cappadocica* might later enhance the white blossoms of the long-stalked *Prunus* 'Shimidsu'.

Even the difficult-to-place, yellow-cream flowered cherry, 'Ukon' (15×10) is made more telling by giving it the coppery-pink 'Fugenzo' for company and carpeting the ground with self-sown forget-me-nots and wild primroses. This is an underplanting which would succeed either on acid or alkaline soil.

In dealing with evergreens, colour and texture of foliage are important. The yellow hued *Chamaecyparis l.* 'Lutea' (15×6) might look harsh and out of place were not a feathery foliaged variety of bluish tone such as *C. l.* 'Fletcheri' or a dark green, placed near by. Coloured foliage must be treated with restraint in naturalistic plantings. I used to dislike variegated forms and felt that evergreys such as *Senecio greyi* (4×4) and lavender looked truly at home only on hot, sunny banks or terraces, but have since come to appreciate their bright appeal in the year-round scheme. Many grey foliaged shrubs, being slightly tender, are only satisfactorily winter hardy in such situations. On the other hand many of the South American evergreens such as *Trieuspidaria lanceolata* (10 × 8—requiring shelter) with its dark, pointed leaves and rosy lanterns, and the not-fully-hardy, pillar-like embothriums (25 × 12) with their tomato-scarlet, honeysuckle-flowers seem to me quite at home among rhododendrons and heaths where I know many shrub gardeners feel uneasy at using them. Much is a matter of taste, yet I do feel that variegated foliage and that of the so-called 'red' leafed species, such as *Prunus cerasifera* 'Nigra' (20 × 6) and *Acer palmatum* 'Atropurpureum', while having a definite place in the formal border, is out of key in an informal planting.

Shape is almost as important as colour. Spire-like evergreens such as the Irish juniper and many of the cypresses should be placed beside a contrasting form such as *A. p.* 'Dissectum' or a low, mounded evergreen such as the rhododendron 'Humming Bird'. The thicket-like pernettyas (3 × 4), on a smaller scale, need the contrast of a tree heath such as *Erica lusitanica* (7 × 6—milder districts only) or *E. arborea* 'Alpina' (5 × 6) with their soft, mossy foliage texture to prevent monotony. Throughout the garden, spire in the foreground should be echoed by spire in the middle-distance. Large-mounded shrubs should rise from carpeters with, near by, more upright growers for contrast, while evergreens should run through the border or glade to give permanent form, at the same time their solid masses being lightened by the lighter effect of deciduous shrubs among them.

I do not think the formal double *Prunus* 'Kiku-shidare Sakura' (syn. *P. serrulata rosea*) can ever look right in an informal border or glade. On the other hand the weeping form of the early single Yoshino cherry—*Prunus × yedoensis* 'Shidare Yoshino'. (8 × 6)—or the weeping spring cherry—*Prunus subhirtella* 'Pendula Rosea'—seem both right and natural. So do the summer brooms—*Genista cinerea* (8 × 6) and *G. aetnensis*—cascading above a hydrangea or medium-growing rhododendron. So much depends on whether the weeping form is natural or artificial in its effect and on whether the blooms have the natural airiness and lightness of the species or whether they give the more formal effect of a man-made hybrid.

I would not, however, wish to exclude hybrids from the in-formal shrub garden. Many, such as *Rhododendron* 'Fastuosum

Flore Pleno' (6×7); the lilac 'Countess of Athlone' (7×7); 'Susan' or 'Blue Peter' with their unostentatious flowers and smoky colouring are not out of place even in woodland. It is rather the artificial colouring, the too formal bloom, and rigid unnatural growth against which one must guard if one strives for a natural scheme.

An informal garden may often be arranged in the form of a glade or series of glades, leading one to the other. Even in a quarter-acre garden, two or three modest glades are possible. A garden glade consists of a long, narrow lawn with curving sweeps of shrubs on either side. Where there is room, one glade may lead into another—or, in a wide garden, two glades, side by side, may be separated by an island bed.

In the beds, the shrubs should be arranged in tiers. The tendency to arrange a shrub-bed in an informal garden like a straight-edged herbaceous border should be resisted. Trees and shrubs should merge into each other as in natural woodland. Standard trees, tall shrubs such as *Genista aetnensis*, and the bigger shrub roses at the back, should shade the intermediate bushes of hydrangea, rhododendron, etc., while dwarf shrubs should be brought to form bays and promontories at the front, interspersed with an under-planting of suitable herbaceous plants, such as lungworts and hellebores, and bulbs. This gradation by height need not, of course, be rigid. It is more effective if here and there a small tree such as *Prunus* 'Amanogawa' or a large shrub like the *Philadelphus* 'Belle Etoile' (5×3) is brought to the front.

A more open scheme may be used in the garden surrounding a bungalow or small house where overshadowing by trees is not wanted. Here paths may take the place of glades, with close-boskaged beds of low shrubs rising on either side. Such shrubs as the heaths, dwarf azaleas, andromeda, helianthemums, small rhododendrons, candytuft, dwarf lavender, prostrate brooms, litho-spermums, the mat-forming *Rosmarinus lavandulaceus* (1×3), etc., would be suitable according to the nature of the soil. These shrublets knit together to form a complete evergreen and floriferous ground cover. Behind rise small shrubs. Paths wind between the shrub-beds perhaps to open into a small lawn, surrounded by favourite shrubs, a tree or two, and underplantings of hellebores, *Geranium endressi,* iris species, bulbs, etc. Sometimes the lawn might be replaced by a natural-looking pool. This type of garden admirably combines rock effects—with big boulders used as outcrops to give root-run to the daphnes, small rhododendrons, azaleas, and helianthemums and to provide backgrounds for lithospermum, dwarf broom, and heaths—shrub-plantings, lawn, and pool, and if a natural stream is present so much the better because running water enhances any garden.

With its small lawn areas and extensive ground cover, a garden such as this is labour-saving; and by careful choice of shrubs and underplanting it can be eye-catching at any time of the year.

Colour schemes are important. In an informal shrub garden, particularly, I think it is important to avoid startling colour contrasts. Harebell blues, pale yellow and white associate well. Yellow and white are good on their own. Pink is pretty with lilac and white. Tomato scarlets of the kind found in the Chilean embothrium and in some rhododendrons may be blended into the garden scheme by juxtapositioning with soft yellow and apricot. Otherwise they must be used on their own against a green background. All other reds must be kept out of eyeshot. The gentle flower tones of some of the shrub and old roses and the dove-grey foliage of *Rosa rubrifolia* are useful to blend in with the summer picture. One of the most pleasing schemes in my present garden consists of the frothy lacecap *Viburnum tomentosum* 'Rowallane' with the early sulphur yellow *Rosa* 'Frühlingsgold' and the soft pink *R. rugosa* hybrid 'Sarah van Fleet' nearby.

'Sarah van Fleet' would be too formal to use in the semi-wild parts of a large garden but in a small garden formality and informality are relative only—and within the closer confines of a more limited space this easy and attractive rose fits in well.

6

Shelter

Many gardeners who might otherwise become shrub-enthusiasts hesitate because they feel that their site is not suited to the growing of shrubs. In the district where I live, within a mile of the sea, I have heard it said, time and again: 'Of course I love lilacs (or rhododendrons, or flowering cherries, or azaleas as the case may be) but what is the use of planting trees and shrubs when my garden is so windy?'

Such misgivings are unnecessary. Experience has proved that shrubs will stand up to coastal winds far better than will herbaceous perennials. Bedding-plants may be blown out of the ground by the gales but flowering shrubs show only a tattered leaf or two and rapidly recover to bloom as usual.

In a windy situation, however, it is necessary to obtain the maximum possible wind-shelter from one's hedges or from wattle or interlap fencing, and in bigger gardens from shelter-belts of evergreen trees. Hedges and wattle fencing are better than walls and interlap fencing because they allow wind and frost to filter through, whereas wind may strike a wall or fence barrier only to swoop over and cause a violent eddy on the other side. Frost, too, must be allowed drainage or serious damage may result.

In really windy gardens, fast-growing hedges up to eight feet in height are necessary to provide protection. The owner of a shrub garden need not be afraid of the resultant shady patches. Many of the best shrubs and ground-cover plants thrive in partial shade.

Cupressus macrocarpa may prove satisfactory as a hedging-plant in sheltered gardens near the sea but it is not reliable for general use. There is available a bi-generic hybrid between this species and the bone-hardy *Chamaecyparis nootkatensis* known as × *Cupressocyparis leylandii*. Opinion differs as to its value as a hedge-plant. As a closely planted shelter-belt it is superb, withstanding severe gales and having attractive foliage which is nearer its *Cupressus macrocarpa* parent in type. It is hardy over southern England and the Midlands, but so far as I know has not been extensively tried in the North. In my opinion it is worth the trial. It does not transplant quite as easily as *Chamaecyparis lawsoniana* but is a better mover than *Cupressus macrocarpa* and may be obtained from specialist nurserymen as reasonably sized (but alas fairly expensive) plants. Some authorities warn that it will not stand clipping but many have found that it stands clipping very well. If planted three to four feet apart as a hedge, the tops must be removed each May and at the same time it may receive the necessary trimming and tapering to keep it within bounds. On the other hand it should not be subjected to twice or thrice yearly clipping after the style of privet.

Chamaecyparis lawsoniana especially in its variety 'Green Hedger' will make a slower growing but reliable hedge. The same rule as to clipping applies to this also but the tops should be left on until the hedge reaches the desired height.

For gardens on the sea-front where hedge-plants are subjected to salt-spray as well as to wind, a spray-resistant hedging-subject must be found. Tamarix is often recommended for the purpose but it is not evergreen and so does not provide adequate shelter in winter—the time when it is most needed. The same objection applies to *Hippophae rhamnoides,* the sea buckthorn, attractive though it may be with its shaggy, silvery foliage and yellow berries (it only berries when both male and female forms are planted, by the way).

Griselinia littoralis is a glossy evergreen with fresh, bright foliage which will stand up to spray and provide a first line of defence against salt-laden winds. *Hebe (Veronica) salicifolia* is another evergreen of attractive appearance which I have found satisfactory. Not hardy in many inland districts, it is a universal sea-side shrub with pleasant willowy leaves and somewhat heath-like flowers of white, or shades of mauve. It is not a startling beauty but it has a quiet charm when grown as a hedge- or shelter-plant.

Escallonia macrantha is probably the best sea-side hedging-shrub of all. This is the Chilean gum-box with glossy, dark green foliage as handsome, though smaller, as that of a camellia. It bears sprays of rosy-red flowers in June and again in November provided that it is clipped immediately after its first flowering and not later in the summer. Moreover it will withstand the full assault of the sea-wind. In gardens on the exposed cliffs of the Great Orme's Head and other exposed parts of the North Wales coast, it thrives and forms dense shelter-hedges. Unfortunately it is not hardy all over the country and in cold districts such as parts of the Thames Valley and in northern inland districts it may even need the protection of a wall. In most southern and western districts, however, it will do well.

Wind, of course, is not such a major problem in all gardens and in many districts one can afford to choose hedges for their background value as much as for the protection they offer.

In my opinion neither *Chamaecyparis* 'Green Hedger' nor *Escallonia macrantha* (for the sea-side and milder districts only) can be bettered as background hedges. But many people prefer hedges which can be kept at a lower height and which take up less room. Holly is slow growing, neat, and attractive and provides a perfect background for a formal garden. It does, however, get very big in time. It is suitable for a five-foot hedge but will not be satisfactory if kept to under three. In its place *Berberis darwinii* might be tried. This is an evergreen shrub with small, holly-like leaves and short, drooping racemes of pretty, orange bells in spring. *B. darwinii* stands clipping well. I know of a hedge which is at least twenty years old and is now no more than two feet in height and is less than a foot in width. Yet it flowers freely and is well furnished to the base.

Beech and hornbeam, though not evergreen, hold their brown leaves through the winter and make a good wind-barrier. They are more suitable for an informal garden than a formal one, and add a touch of warm brown to the winter landscape. The only fault is that they are among the latest shrubs to come into spring leaf and so should not be planted where they can be seen from the main windows of the house.

Our front garden is hedged with beech. We enjoy its cosy brown in winter and the tender green of its spring leaves at bluebell-time but not a spring goes by without our wondering exasperatedly when, if ever, it will come into leaf. Always it seems a full month behind other deciduous hedges.

If beech and hornbeam hedges are to retain their leaves during the winter months they should be clipped no earlier or later than August. For a cold district or a clay soil, hornbeam is preferable.

Some people prefer a flowering hedge. One of the best flowering evergreens is *Berberis* × *stenophylla*—lovely in spring when its sprays of golden flowers shower the dark foliage, but it needs a lot of room as too much clipping spoils the flower-display. For the really small garden *B. darwinii*, which I mentioned earlier, is the better plant.

On acid soil, the early-flowering *Rhododendron* × *praecox* makes a beautiful hedge with neat, small leaves and pinkish-mauve, funnel-shaped flowers in February and March. This rhododendron is sometimes only semi-evergreen in the open garden, but it seems to hold its leaves better as a hedge. It is completely hardy and need not be as extravagant a proposition as it sounds. In 1959 I bought from a Derbyshire nursery, good twelve- to fifteen-inch plants at under five shillings each. (All costs have, of course, gone up but the same nursery is still reasonable in its prices.) The rhododendron 'Blue Diamond' is a somewhat slower grower that may be used to make thick and colourful hedges within the garden. With neat, dark foliage and deep blue flowers in May it would be particularly pleasing to enclose one of those 'gardens within a garden' discussed in Chapter 2. Both 'Blue Diamond' and *R.* × *praecox* should be planted two feet apart and may be cut back should they become too high.

Tree heaths make most attractive hedges in country districts and although they are slow-growing at first they eventually make splendid, dense, evergreen boundaries with attractive, and often scented, flowers to boot. They are particularly effective set on top of a bank and may be varied by interplanting with the double-flowered, apricot-scented gorse—*Ulex europaeus* 'Plenus'.

One of the best heaths for acid soils is the hawthorn-scented *Erica arborea* 'Alpina' with bright mossy-green foliage and ash-white flowers in spring. It is hardy in most districts.

If you want a rosy-purple heath, there is *E. mediterranea* 'Superba' whose distinctive flowers are much more showy than those of the type and honey-scented. It will make a four- or five-foot hedge in time. Accommodating even on alkaline soils, *E. stricta*, the autumn-flowering, Corsican heath will grow to five feet or more in height. It bears a profusion of pleasing pink bells at the ends of its shoots in August and September with a later sprinkling, and retains the flowers, turned to foxy-russet, through the winter. It is useful also to make a distinctive hedge within the garden itself and at Bodnant such a hedge forms an informal background for the large lily pool.

For sheltered places *Choisya ternata*, the Mexican orange-blossom, is a charming hedging-subject which will reach to five or six feet in time. It has distinctive and pleasing three-lobed leaves and carries its sweetly scented white flowers in bursts from May to September. Unfortunately it will not stand wind and is, therefore, more suited to form a division within the garden rather than a boundary hedge.

Another scented, slightly tender shrub which makes an attractive hedge is *Osmanthus delavayi*. This is truly hardy only in the South and West or near the coast. However it is a plant of such distinction with small, neat leaves and vanilla-scented, tubular, white spring flowers that it should be used in any suitable locality. Like the choisya, its main enemy is wind. I have had young plants browned and cut back by a strong south-westerly wind, so for this and for other choice wind-tender plants, such as the vulnerable winter-flowering *Camellia sasanqua*, it is worth erecting temporary wind-screens of wattle or hessian until the plants become well established.

A bi-generic hybrid between the osmanthus and *Phillyrea decora*, × *Osmarea burkwoodii*, is almost as good and is decidedly hardier than *Osmanthus delavayi*.

You will notice that I have recommended as hedging-shrubs only those plants which keep their leaves throughout the winter. In my opinion the shrub garden should look attractive and well furnished throughout the year and, therefore, it would be a mistake to plant a leaf-losing hedge which would present only a bare, bleak appearance from November to April. An evergreen hedge, or one which at least retains its coloured leaves in the way of beech and hornbeam, is always pleasant to look at and provides protection for the garden the year round.

In the larger garden of half an acre or more there will often be room for a screen of evergreen trees to break the force of the prevailing wind. Even here, the Scotch fir, chosen for the purpose in big gardens, would be out of scale. Varieties of *Chamaecyparis lawsoniana* or X *Cupressocyparis leylandii*, spaced at seven feet and unclipped, would prove more suitable, and more effective as they remain well furnished to the base. One or two plants with coloured foliage such as the bluish *Chamaecyparis l.* 'Fletcheri' or the golden *C. l.* 'Stewartii' could well be included with the *C. lawsoniana* to give liveliness and variety to the scene, although the cupressocyparis being quicker growing should be planted on its own. To mix it with the *C. lawsoniana* varieties could lead only to a ragged effect.

In a country situation mixed hedges can be very effective. In one garden I designed, we planted *Elaeagnus* X *ebbingei* at three-foot intervals interspersed with the red floribunda rose 'Frensham'. Although this rose is normally subject to black spot, the elaeagnus foliage seemed to protect it from the fungus. Furthermore, this trouble is now easily controllable by spraying with the systemic fungicide 'Benlate'. The ugly winter legginess of the rose was effectively hidden by the elaeagnus.

7

Trees for the Small Garden

Trees for the small shrub garden must be carefully chosen or they will be out of scale and sooner or later outgrow their position. They are essential to give shade, which many choicer shrubs and underlings need, and also to add height and variety to the plantings.

One of the most delightful small trees for a formal part of the garden is quite undistinguished in flower but its habit and foliage render it wholly desirable. It is the weeping, willow-leafed pear— *Pyrus salicifolia* 'Pendula' (8×6)—which forms a picturesquely gnarled tree that may after many years become fifteen feet high and perhaps eight feet across. Its slender, willow-like leaves are silvered and its branches arch gracefully from its sturdy trunk. Near a path or at the edge of paving it is one of the most charming small trees I know and its silver-grey leaves give it an air of quiet dignity that fit it for such an important position.

Flowering cherries are probably the most popular of all trees for the small garden, and of them *Prunus subhirtella* 'Autumnalis' (15×10) is indispensable. I have sometimes heard it said that the pink variety, *P. s. a.* 'Rosea', of this autumn- and winter-blooming tree is less free-flowering than the type but never in my own experience have I found this to be the case. The blossom of the tree in our own garden is pink and, like many others that I know in this part of North Wales, it flowers unfailingly in November and again in any mild spell the winter through. In March it provides a display that is only equalled by a selected, and very floriferous form of the spring cherry—*P. subhirtella*

'Beni Higan' (15 × 8). In larger gardens both *P. s.* 'Autumnalis' and 'Beni Higan' should be grown. Where there is room for only one early cherry the display may safely be left to *P. s.* 'Autumnalis'.

Prunus 'Amanogawa', the maypole cherry, is particularly useful where space is short. It is slender and upright as a small poplar and should always be planted at the front of the border so that its blossom-wreathed stem may be revealed. Incidentally, never purchase a plant of this cherry which is not 'feathered' with branches to the base. With its scented, semi-double, pale pink flowers in late April, 'Amanogawa' is the spring tree *par excellence* for the small garden. Yet it is not often seen, many people preferring to plant the cruder pink, ubiquitous 'Kanzan' which, though lovely as an adult tree, is too big for any garden under a quarter of an acre and so often has to submit to mutilating pruning while it is still in the inverted-umbrella stage and before it attains the dignity of its spreading maturity. Its place may well be taken by *P. s.* 'Pink Perfection' (12 × 8) which is a better colour and a much less vigorous tree.

Where there is space for a selection of flowering cherries I would suggest the inclusion of the March-flowering, delicately blush coloured, single *P. × yedoensis*. The type may in time have a spread of twenty-five feet, so for the small garden the weeping form—*P. × y.* 'Shidare Yoshino' (12 × 8)—may be the wiser choice.

'Okamé' (15 × 8) is one of the newer hybrid cherries raised in this country by Captain Collingwood Ingram who has done so much work on the genus. It makes a small tree with deep rosy-pink single flowers prodigally carried on slender brown shoots. It is one of the very best flowering cherries and it should be included wherever there is room. 'Okamé' has an ultimate spread of about eighteen feet; yet even eighteen feet may sound alarming to the gardener with only a small plot of ground. However it should be realized that shallow-rooted shrubs such as the rhododendron hybrids or deciduous azaleas may be planted almost up to the trunk of a standard cherry without harm.

Towards the end of April, or early in May, 'Mikuruma-gaeshi' (*P. diversiflora*) (15 × 10) flowers. This is a tree of restricted spread. Its long branches are ascending in form, giving a vase-shaped outline which is lovely when clothed with the clusters of large, shapely, single, blush-pink flowers.

The beauty of this cherry is expressed in its Japanese name—'Mikuruma-gaeshi'—which means 'the royal carriage returns'. The legend runs that when the Emperor first saw this cherry he was so struck by its loveliness that he stopped his carriage and went back to look at the cherry more closely.

My favourite cherry is one of the latest to flower—the frilly, white 'Shimidsu Sakura' (*P. serrulata longipes*) which blooms in May and lasts long in blossom.

After the cherries the crab-apples. Of these probably the best for the small garden is the pink and white *Malus floribunda* (20 × 12) with its attractive, arching branches. Many people like the crimson flowered varieties but unfortunately this deep colouring is often associated with muddy purple leaves which never look right in the informal garden. In a formal garden, coloured leaves may be permissibly used for contrast effects but even here such effects may better be obtained by the livelier red foliage of the double, pink, apricot hybrid *Prunus × blireiana* (12 × 6).

A red (or near-red) flowered crab-apple which has green foliage is *Malus atrosanguinea* (20 × 12)—often incorrectly listed as a variety of *M. floribunda*. *M. atrosanguinea* and *M. floribunda* are similar in habit, both forming small, mushroom-headed trees. But, to my mind, *M. atrosanguinea* in spite of its deeper colouring, does not have the same charm as *M. floribunda* whose crimson buds and blush-white flowers have a bridal gaiety that seems in keeping with the spirit of the spring garden.

I hesitate to recommend either almond or peach trees for the really small garden. Both are less effective than the early cherries and both are subject to disfiguring attacks of leaf-curl which may, however, be treated by a spray of lime-sulphur in the early bud stage or by spraying with nicotine when the blight appears. The only almond which really has a place in the small garden is the dwarf Russian almond—*Prunus tenella*—which is shrubby in habit and forms a thicket of three-foot stems that become freely wreathed with bright pink single flowers in spring. This shrubby almond looks particularly lovely above a carpet of muscari or

Anemone apennina. Prunus tenella 'Fire Hill Form' is the most vivid with deep red buds opening to crimson-pink blossoms.

I am never sure whether lilacs should be reckoned as trees or shrubs but as many of them become tree-like in time I will include them here. Most of the named hybrids are good. Which you select depends on your personal taste as regards colour, size of bloom, and whether you prefer single or double flowers. The hybrid lilacs are essentially trees for formal parts of the garden. Lilacs we all must have, if only for the nostalgia of their scent. But for the informal shrub garden I think I would choose the species with their smaller flowers and flower-trusses, more graceful habit, and even finer scent. The Persian lilac—*Syringa persica* (15×4)—which comes, oddly enough, from China is one of the best. More shrubby than tree-like, it has slender, narrow leaves and trusses of fragrant, lavender coloured flowers. Useful, too, is *S. microphylla* 'Superba' (8×8) which flowers twice, in spring and later, and is so frequently in bloom in the late autumn that one nurseryman at least lists it as a winter-flowering shrub. It is a delicately pretty little shrub with large panicles of dainty pink flowers.

Many gardeners feel that a garden is not a garden for them unless it includes at least one laburnum. *Laburnum alpinum* (25×18) probably makes the most handsome, strongly growing tree, but for the small garden where space is limited *L. × vossii* (15×15) or *L. × watereri* (15×15) would be more suitable with their less vigorous and more upright growth and longer chains of bloom.

Whether or not you are a laburnum fan, the embothrium is the tree to which you will aspire if you want a real garden and are prepared to take trouble to achieve it. Nothing is more brilliant than the slender flame of the Chilean fire-bush flaunting its tomato-scarlet flowers against the green background of cypress or yew. Yet the embothrium with its vivid, honeysuckle flowers and evergreen leaves is seen in comparatively few gardens. This may be because the earlier species introduced to this country were decidedly tender. But in *Embothrium lanceolatum* 'Norquinço Valley Form' we have a tree that is hardy enough for most gardens south of the Trent or near the west coast. It needs care in siting, away from cutting easterly winds and not in too dry or sun-baked a spot. Rhododendron conditions of a moist, well-drained, humus-containing soil suit it best and it is reputed to dislike lime. Some of the earlier forms were not very free-flowering but the 'Norquinço Valley Form' flowers with prodigality, the flower-clusters almost touching one another so that the whole branch seems clothed in scarlet. Because it is a rapid grower the embothrium should be carefully staked, secured by a rubber collar, and guyed to guard against wind-rock. It may reach twenty feet or more in height over the years but its slim growth takes up very little space, mature specimens occupying less room than a vase-trained pear tree.

The cercis is another lovely subject that is too often neglected in gardens. I have seen it stated by a reputable authority that the Judas tree—*Cercis siliquastrum* (10 × 6)—will flower freely only in sunny spots in southern gardens, but my experience does not bear that out.

Here, in North Wales, which although mild in winter cannot be said to be either hot or particularly sunny in summer, many gardens boast Judas trees which flower magnificently every year. Some of these are situated in shady and far from sun-baked positions where every May their bare branches become wreathed in rosy coloured pea flowers, giving them the appearance of a giant *Daphne mezereum*. The heart-shaped leaves usually colour splendidly in the autumn.

The Judas tree is quite hardy enough to grow well near Manchester but its branches are rather brittle and it will not stand much wind. It should, therefore, be given a sheltered position and should be planted out when young. About two feet is the usual height and young trees this size, though formerly remarkably cheap to buy, can still be obtained from £2–£3 each—little enough for a lifetime of beauty. Owing to its habit of forking near the ground the Judas tree may in time sprawl over a considerable area. This may easily be prevented, as it does not resent pruning, by removing any branches with a sprawling tendency and restricting the tree to a main stem when young.

Another little-known tree is one of the June highlights in the lives of those gardeners who grow it. The snowdrop tree—*Styrax japonica* (8×8)—was formerly thought to need woodland conditions to do well. It is, however, quite hardy but it does like semi-shade and it dislikes lime. *S. japonica* is usually seen as a small spreading tree of eight or nine feet high. It has pleasant dark green leaves and in June its elegant branches are hung with myriads of white bells like upside-down snowdrops.

The summer-blooming magnolias flower in June with pendant, white, claret or crimson centred cup-shaped flowers. In appearance the flowers are quite different from the upright chalices of the spring-blooming group but, nevertheless, with their solid waxy petals and haunting scent, they have the unmistakable distinction of the genus.

Magnolia sieboldii (parviflora) (8×10) is the one most commonly seen. It is a sprawling tree which can only be kept within bounds by the occasional pruning away of the oldest branches at ground-level. It bears a flower-crop in May and goes on blooming slightly less freely until August. Like the styrax it dislikes lime.

For alkaline soil, *M. sieboldii*'s Chinese cousin *M. sinensis* (8×10) is the species to choose. Its waxy-white, bowl-shaped flowers with their central club of stamens and carpels, are similar but more pendant. This species does not have such a long-flowering season as *M. sieboldii* but its fruits are of a decorative bright crimson and it is a very desirable plant although apt to sprawl and needing restricting pruning to confine it to its allotted space.

M. wilsonii (8×5) is again similar but with narrower leaves and attractively furred young shoots which may make the anxious but inexperienced gardener believe that its spring growth has been frosted until he sees the buds unfurl. It is more upright and less spreading in habit than the other two and so is perhaps better suited to the small garden.

Of the spring-flowering section of the genus two types are suitable for the average garden. The first, *M. stellata*, the starry magnolia, is more of a shrub than a tree with characteristic, dark barked, twiggy growth. It seldom reaches more than ten feet high even after many years. With its angled branches it has a strongly Japanese appearance and is a most desirable and distinctive shrub. Unfortunately it has been scarce in commerce of late. This is said to be due to its dislike of moving—a plea which frankly I cannot understand. Rather do I think the trouble lies with imported plants—reared in Holland for the greenhouse trade and grown almost entirely in peat—being planted without due preparation into inhospitable soil. A shovelful or two of peat around the roots at planting as well as a further sprinkling mixed with the surrounding soil would, I am sure, solve the problem. We almost lost a *M. stellata* in our garden in 1959 and wondered whether it was due to belated resentment of moving. On digging it up it was found that a maidenhair fern had seriously encroached into its roots. The fern was disentangled and removed, the magnolia moved to another part of the garden and replanted, and far from resenting the move it has thrived with increased vigour.

There are several other distinctive magnolias in the spring-flowering section such as *M. salicifolia* and *M. kobus*. Neither of these, however, flower for some years and they eventually make large trees whereas *M. stellata* blooms when only a foot high.

Many of the chalice-flowered magnolias are too big for the average garden. Some such as the great *M. campbelli*, *M. sprengeri*, *M. sargentiana robusta*, and *M. mollicomata* need the favoured conditions of those south-west and western gardens whose climates are regulated by the nearness of the Gulf Stream. Even there *M. campbelli* will be frosted in three years out of five. In the small garden the place of these giants must be taken by the shrubby hybrid *M. × soulangiana* and its varieties. *M. × soulangiana* (10 × 8) makes a widely spreading bushy tree, similar in habit to the Judas tree. It should be planted in paving or grass where it has room to complete its spread. Its flowers are chalice-shaped, flushed with purple on the outside and white within. Although not as glamorous as the great tree magnolias of the West it is none the less a good plant and is, in fact, the one most commonly seen. Better, in my opinion, and with its more upright growth, more suited to a place in the small garden glade is *M. × s.* 'Lennei' (10 × 6) of similar parentage to *M. × soulangiana* but with blooms that are only a few degrees less lovely than those of *M. campbelli* itself. *M. × s.* 'Lennei' bears huge goblets of rosy-purple that are waxy-white within. Like *M. × soulangiana* it flowers when only two feet high. Equally lovely is *M. × s.* 'Alba Superba' (8 × 6) with pure white flowers. *M. × s.* 'Rustica Rubra' (10 × 6) is another ·of this group with blooms half-way between those of *M. soulangiana* and *M. × s.* 'Lennei', heavily flushed on the outside with rose and purple while *M. × s.* 'Alexandrina' (10 × 6) is white softly flushed with pink.

To return to summer-flowering trees, the only subjects of real note for August are the eucryphias, and, lovely though these are, the only one which is not too big for the small garden is *Eucryphia glutinosa* (*pinnatifolia*) (7 × 6); and its beautiful white saucer-shaped, Rose of Sharon flowers with their freckling of crimson anthers are too soon over to really pay for the space it occupies. For bigger gardens, however, this eucryphia is a *must*. Its habit is often bushy and spreading but it can be trained to columnar growth and its fresh green, pinnate foliage is most attractive. Its distinguished offspring 'Nymansay' (20 × 8) is evergreen and thereby misses the autumn fires of scarlet, amber, and gold which burn the dying foliage of *E. glutinosa*. Its flowers, which are more like those of its other parent, the tender, evergreen *E. cordifolia* are borne for a longer period, although to my mind they have not quite the same delicate beauty as those of *E. glutinosa*. 'Nymansay' is a columnar grower but reaches thirty to forty feet in time and so is quite unsuitable for any garden under an acre in size where the smaller 'Rostrevor' would suit better.

The rowan, or mountain ash, *Sorbus aucuparia* (15 × 8) is one of the most decorative, berry-bearing trees in existence. I like to see it in a shrub garden but some people, I know, feel it is too much a plant of the wild hedgerows to be given garden space. It is, too, a sizeable grower and its place might well be taken by *S. hupehensis* (12 × 5)—a smaller, more slender-growing tree. In early autumn *S. hupehensis* bears immense clusters of pure white fruits which later become flushed with rose and last well into the winter.

Forest trees are out of place in the small garden but our native silver birch (25 × 10) is a graceful woodlander which looks right anywhere with its airy leaves and silver bark. The golden glory of its autumn foliage is unsurpassed but I like best to see it in spring, rising from a drift of heaths or planted in rough grass with bluebells and wild daffodils for its companions.

In the small garden every tree must either flower or else have beauty of foliage, form, and bark to recommend it. Into this latter category comes *Acer griseum* (15 × 8) the paper-bark maple, not only for the beauty of its tattered cinnamon coloured bark but also for the warm orange to which its leaves colour in autumn. 'Osakazuki' (7 × 5) has the most brilliant autumn colour of all the maples—an unmatched blood-crimson—while the seven-lobed leaves of *A*. 'Heptalobum Elegans' (8 × 6) not only colour brilliantly in autumn but have an attractive bronzy cast over their green throughout the summer.

The stewartias (10 × 5) too are noted for autumn colour and although small and slender in growth have a distinctly tree-like habit and a most attractive port—what many of us think of as 'the Japanese look' in fact. Unfortunately they are suitable only for reasonably sheltered gardens on acid soil. They bear white flowers throughout July and August and have prettily peeling, pinky-grey bark. *Stewartia pseudo-camellia* is one of the most beautiful with cup-shaped, snow-white flowers centred by bright yellow anthers. *S. serrata* is good, too, with creamy flowers tinged with red at the base while the Chinese species *S. sinensis* adds flower-scent to its many charms.

Although often of large size, the birches are too beautiful entirely to neglect. For the golden shower of its autumn leaves and the frosty beauty of its bark in winter, the silver birch deserves a place in any informal part of the shrub garden where room can be found. It associates well with heathers or other low growing plants. Care must be taken to keep its beautiful trunk clear of all intrusive foliage.

Many of the eucalyptus species have beautiful bark and leaves. One of the hardiest is *E. niphophila*—the Snow Gum—(12 × 6) which can be kept small by pruning. This will encourage the production of its very decorative young leaves for flower arrangements. Whenever possible it should be cut so as to reveal its beautiful trunk.

8

Small and Medium Rhododendrons

Most rhododendrons dislike an alkaline soil and many gardeners whose land is situated upon limestone or chalk find this a keen disappointment. It is no small hardship to have to forgo one of the loveliest of all genera.

Fortunately not all rhododendrons dislike lime equally and whereas admittedly they could not be grown in a chalk-pit, many deciduous rhododendron species (the deciduous azaleas and the winter-flowering *Rhododendron dauricum* and *R. mucronulatum*) and most small-leafed species can, with care, be grown reasonably well where the soil is slightly alkaline provided that they are planted in a compost of peat and rotted bracken with a little cow-manure for extra nutriment. The acid content of the soil should be supplemented by mulching with chopped green bracken each June. Formerly leaf-mould was used to mulch rhododendrons but this practice has been found unsatisfactory as most leaf-mould has a surprisingly high alkaline content.

We experimented for some years with rhododendrons and other lime-hating plants in our own garden where, although the soil is definitely on the alkaline side of neutral, azaleas (both evergreen and deciduous), small-leafed rhododendrons, and camellias grow happily in the bracken peat compost recommended earlier. Larger leafed rhododendrons of the hardy hybrid type and the *R. campylocarpum* and *R. griersonianum* hybrids present more of a problem and, although they grow and flower reasonably well, a slight chlorosis, or yellowing, of the leaves show that they are deficient of some essential nutriment.

As is well known the presence of calcium in the soil prevents the uptake of iron by plants. Moreover some plants—particularly the members of the Ericaceae family—need more iron than others. Even in the same genus differences exist in this respect and some rhododendrons need to take up quite large quantitities of iron from the soil whilst others (the small-leafed and deciduous types in particular) can do with very little.

A product known as Sequestrene Iron was introduced some years ago. It consisted of iron in a form which could be absorbed by plants growing in some alkaline soils. Unfortunately it was not stable in alkaline clays—and many gardens where the soil is alkaline, including ours, have a clay sub-soil. The Geigy Company then introduced Chel DP Iron which they claimed was stable in alkaline soils and which has been widely and successfully tested on fruit trees. Welcomed enthusiastically, it was tried out in gardens up and down the country by volunteers who wanted to grow lime-hating plants in soils of alkaline clay—it is one of the facts of life that almost everybody who begins to garden on lime or chalk immediately yearns to grow rhododendrons, azaleas, *Gentiana sino-ornata,* and other forbidden joys. I tried Chel DP Iron in our garden (our soil is in some parts neutral, pH 7, and in others on the alkaline side of neutral with a pH rating of 7·5) where several rhododendrons were showing chlorotic symptoms (yellowing of the leaves between the veins). A badly chlorotic young plant of *R. orbiculare* responded so well to a sixteenth of an ounce of Chel DP Iron, watered well in, that the yellow leaves became deep green within a month. Other plants were slower to respond. Five-year-old layers of the *R. griersonianum* hybrids 'Fabia "Roman Pottery"' and 'Goblin' treated in early April with half an ounce of Chel DP Iron each showed little result until they sent up new growth in June. The new growth was a healthy dark green and the old leaves gradually deepened in colour and were retained. *R. campylocarpum* hybrids 'Goldfinch' and 'Carita' responded well as did 'Susan' and the old *R.* 'Fastuosum Flore Pleno'.

The *arboreum* × *caucasicum* hybrid *R.* 'Nobleanum Venustum' which flowers in December with us showed little response so far as leaf colour is concerned, although in a soil of pH 7·5 well mulched with bracken and rhododendron peat and laced with flowers of sulphur (a well-known corrector of alkalinity) it grows and flowers well. The old 'Lady Eleanor Cathcart' (*arboreum × maximum*) showed little response and the same is true of 'Britannia'. Is the common factor here the *R. arboreum* strain? And may rhododendrons of this strain be less able to absorb the Sequestrene than others? Or is some other factor such as deficiency of manganese resulting in an obstinate chlorosis?

Manganese deficiency usually shows itself as chlorosis of the young growth; iron deficiency also causes chlorosis of younger leaves. The rhododendron 'Humming Bird' suffered from definite manganese deficiency. The old leaves became dark olive-green with the Sequestrene treatment, but the young leaves showed an obstinate yellow. A spray of manganese sulphate (one ounce to two and a half gallons of cold water) cured this. So where Sequestrene does not completely clear up any chlorosis, a manganese sulphate spray should be tried.[1]

Some rhododendrons and azaleas are less subject to iron deficiency than others. In my soil, ranging from pH 7 to 7·5, small-leafed and deciduous rhododendrons and azaleas grow freely and without chlorosis. The Lapponicum and Glaucum series of dwarf rhododendrons, together with the deciduous azaleas seem to be singularly trouble-free in this respect. We always plant them in rhododendron peat with which quantities of rotted bracken have been incorporated and take the precaution of lining each planting-hole with flowers of sulphur.

Growing rhododendrons and similar lime-haters in alkaline soils is still, one might say, a risky affair. But the results of my experiments with Sequestrene and manganese sulphate lead me to believe that given proper soil conditions (a spongy peaty compost to enable the iron solution to reach the roots) and good drainage to avoid root troubles, one may well succeed. I would advise readers with alkaline soil to proceed cautiously, trying one or two plants at first before indulging in heavy expenditure on shrubs which might not succeed. With the dwarf rhododendrons and azaleas I think one can be reasonably sure of success provided

[1] See note on page 74.

they are planted in acid rhododendron peat, kept mulched with either acid peat or bracken and planted in holes lined with flowers of sulphur. A word of warning should perhaps be given regarding the source of peat. Readers with access to peat-holes on moorlands or mountains should not apply such peat to their gardens until it has weathered for at least six months and been well mixed with sand. Freshly dug peat is so acid that it may well kill even lime-haters unless it is treated in this way.

The manufacture of Chel DP Iron was taken over by Murphy Chemical Co. and is now available as Murphy Sequestrene with added manganese and magnesium.

Apart from the special needs of alkaline soils, rhododendrons and azaleas need thorough soil preparation if they are to give of their best. Heavy soils should be lightened with sand and peat while light sandy soils need the addition of peat, compost, and strawy cow-manure to give them body and help them to retain moisture.

With the exception of some of the large-leafed giants, rhodo-dendrons do not like too wet a position and their roots must never be waterlogged. Good drainage is essential. A medium loam with added peat or rotted bracken suits rhododendrons best, especially if the humus content and acidity are kept high by an annual mulch of bracken cut green in June as suggested earlier. Particular care must be taken not to plant too deeply but at the exact level at which the soil-mark shows the shrubs to have been growing in the nursery. Nor should the soil be trampled down too firmly near to the stem. I like to plant with only peat above the root-ball, so as to allow the roots to breathe. In fact I line the planting-hole with peat and also mix peat well into the surrounding soil so as to give the roots congenial conditions in which to spread. Shrubs of the rhododendron, camellia, magnolia, and allied types are very reluctant to thrust their roots into sticky hostile soil and so a generous interlacing of peat persuades them to make the adjust-ment. Rhododendrons need regular mulching and if bracken is not available one should use a proper grade of rhododendron peat. I emphasize rhododendron peat because much horticultural peat has been neutralized for vegetable-growing and so is not sufficiently acid for rhododendrons. A four-inch layer is not too much but care must be taken to keep the mulch away from the stems and to watch that subsequent watering does not wash the mulch to the stems and impact it there. If this happens no air can get to the roots and so the plant may die. More rhododendrons are lost through the root-ball being buried too deeply and deprived of air than from any other cause.

A fallacy which dies hard is the widely held belief that it is useless to attempt to grow any but the oh-so-dull hardy hybrids in the average garden. Admittedly only a few of us have woodland gardens. Bodnant and Exbury are not for all, but many of the bluer blooded hybrids and the hardier species can be grown in any but the most exposed gardens provided they are given adequate wind-shelter (this is a very real 'must' for all but the tiny leafed species or hybrids) and shade from the midday sun in the south of the country. (In Wales and the North this shade is not nearly so necessary—in fact in parts of Scotland too much shade reduces flowering very considerably.)

The rhododendron year begins in January when *R. dauricum* and the allied *R. mucronulatum* flower. Both these species need the protection of a north wall or of a sheltering evergreen, or they may be planted beneath the overhead canopy formed by the branches of a taller deciduous tree. Such precautions will help to protect their flowers from frost damage.

R. dauricum is semi-evergreen and more compact than *R. mucronulatum*. It usually makes a rounded, three-foot bush, whereas the deciduous *R. mucronulatum* makes a twiggy, more open shrub of perhaps five feet. Both bear azalea-like flowers of rosy purple in pairs or clusters at the ends of the branches. Those of *R. mucronulatum*, however, are finer and open over a longer period from January or February to March so that if one crop is frosted there are more to come. Both *R. dauricum* and *R. mucronulatum* are attractive and look particularly well when planted near *Hamamelis mollis*.

Many early-flowering rhododendrons, such as the dwarf, milky-white *R. leucaspis* and 'Bric à Brac' whose pink buds open to pure white, dark anthered blooms, are subject to frost damage. We find polythene cloches to be an advantage here. We place them over the plants at night when the buds are opening and remove them during the day except in the most severe weather. This may seem troublesome but it is a trouble well worth taking so that the delightful early flowers may be enjoyed unspoiled.

The tough *R. racemosum* is a little later to flower. With its small leaves and upright racemes of tiny, funnel-shaped flowers it is a neat and attractive plant. The colour of the flowers varies from pale apple-blossom pink to the warm pink of Forrest's dwarf form (two feet high—seed-packet number F19404). Messrs. Cox of Glendoick, Perthshire, the well-known joint-authors of *Modern Rhododendrons*, offered a most desirable, tall-growing form with dark pink flowers. Crossed with the lovely but more tender *R. ciliatum*, *R. racemosum* has given us a free-flowering hybrid 'Racil' which in March or early April bears its larger, funnel-shaped flowers of glowing pink which fade to white.

A hybrid hardy enough for any garden is the March-flowering *R.×praecox*, the result of a cross between *R. dauricum* and *R. ciliatum*. Its pinky-mauve, butterfly flowers are larger than those of *R. dauricum* and it makes a five-foot bush in time. It is very free-flowering. In sheltered gardens *R.×praecox* may be sited near the primrose *R. lutescens* (F.C.C. form) to make a rewarding colour picture. *R. lutescens* is lovely, too, in its own right, its very colour speaking of spring and the returning light, but it is useless for exposed gardens, as is 'Remo' its brighter, smaller-growing off-spring with the choice *R. valentinianum*.

Of all rhododendrons, the species of the dwarf Lapponicum series have the greatest potentialities for drift-planting in the small shrub garden. These little rhododendrons are as hardy as the heather which they replace on the mountains of Asia. They will stand sun and wind and are sturdy small bushes, usually mounded in habit and from two to three feet high with occasional taller exceptions. Their tiny, often aromatic, leaves in the late autumn take on shades of rusty-red, bronze, frosty-emerald, and deep green that make them colourful in the winter garden, and in April clusters of small, open-throated flowers cover the compact plants Many of the Lapponicum series—*R. chryseum, R. intricatum,* and *R. hippophaeoides* among others—bloom for a second time in August.

In colour the rhododendrons of the Lapponicum series range

from white and yellow to rose, rosy-purple, violet, lilac, mauve, and near blue. They should be grouped in a drift behind a patch of late summer-flowering heaths so that their second flowering coincides with the blooming of the heaths.

I like also to see the Lapponicum rhododendrons placed so that the whole group flowers together in spring. *R. intricatum* with its twiggy growth and soft lavender-blue flowers is essential for an April group. With it I would plant the rosy-violet *R. lysolepis*; *R. chryseum* with its red anthered, primrose flowers; the mauve *R. stictophyllum*; *R. impeditum* in its best blue form; the deep, almost sapphire *R. russatum*, and the rosy-purple *R. tapetiforme*.

Several good hybrids exist between the blue Lapponicum series and the larger-flowered, near-blue *R. augustinii* of the *R. triflorum* series. These combine the hardiness of the *R. lapponicum* series with the larger flowers and nearness to blue of the more tender *R. augustinii*.

'Blue Tit' (*impeditum*✕ *augustinii*), 'Blue Diamond' ('Intrifast'✕ *augustinii*), 'Blue Bird' (*intricatum*✕ *augustinii*), and 'Augfast' (*augustinii*✕ *fastigiatum*) are all fine hybrids, rated Category A for hardiness, and with flowers in varying shades of blue. Their flowering season overlaps and in bloom with 'Sapphire' ('Blue Tit'✕ *impeditum*) and 'Intrifast' (*intricatum*✕ *fastigiatum*) they are all so near that one must either plant the whole group, adding *R. williamsianum* or *R. davidsonianum* for contrast (in colder places a good pink *R. racemosum* would be better) or one must confine the planting to a group of one hybrid or use them as individual plants. When we first began our garden my husband and I made the mistake of grouping 'Blue Tit' (late April) and 'Blue Diamond' (early May) together, thinking that they would flower successively. Unfortunately the flowering overlapped and the charming harebell-blue flowers of 'Blue Tit' looked but pale shadows of themselves when the deeper 'Blue Diamond' opened. We later separated them and 'Blue Tit', helped by mound-layering (peat and leaf-mould heaped over the bush so that only the shoots protrude to enable the stems to root along their length) increased so fast that we eventually had enough plants to edge a path in front of some of the larger hybrids.

Later in May the easy-growing *R. saluenense* series offers some useful, dwarf, spreading shrubs for the small garden. The flowers of this series are mostly in shades of magenta-purple but all are showy and attractive and have foliage which is pleasing the year round. *R. calostrotum* is one of the best known. It is a grey foliaged carpeter with large flat flowers of the typical magenta-purple colouring. In winter the leaves take on a colourful reddish tinge which enlivens the garden scene. *R. keleticum* is another of the series, making an almost prostrate, rounded bush with large flowers that are nearer crimson than the purple in which the series specializes. *R. radicans* is a ground-hugging, creeping plant, no more than two inches high but quickly spreading to cover two or more square feet with its neat, little leaves and lowly branches. It carries flowers—big for the size of the plant—which are among the prettiest of the series, nodding and rose-purple. Easy and free-flowering *R. radicans* is one of the best of the smaller rhododendrons. It is splendid at the front of a shrub border or will sprawl over a low rock in the more open type of shrub garden. All these little rhododendrons benefit from being planted among sandstone rocks under which they may get their roots.

R. 'Prostigiatum' is an interesting hybrid between the mat-forming *R. prostratum* of the *R. saluenense* series (with lilac-purple flowers spotted with red) and *R. fastigiatum* of the Lapponicum series. It varies from an almost prostrate form to an upright little bush like *R. fastigiatum* while its flowers range from deep lavender-purple to a pale smoky-mauve. It is one of those plants you must see in flower before you buy to ensure getting the form you like best. Larger-flowered and more brilliant are the free-flowering hybrids of the glorious but shy-flowering, scarlet *R. repens*. 'Elizabeth' (*repens* × *griersonianum*) carries her cherry trumpets freely on a three-foot bush and is one of the most desirable rhododendrons for any small garden with average shade and wind-shelter. Like many *R. griersonianum* crosses, 'Elizabeth' is rather weak in foliage but her flowers are so glamorous as to redeem this fault. For the front row of a shrub border or to drape a rock there is a creeping form of this hybrid known as 'Jenny'. 'Ethel' is between the two in size, and is a bright pink hybrid of similar type ('F.C.

Puddle' × *repens*) while 'Treasure' (*repens* × *williamsianum*) makes a small, spreading shrub with bell-shaped, deep pink flowers.

'Little Bert' and 'Little Ben' are a hardy pair of hybrids with very similar parentage but with the seed and pollen parents reversed which, as is often the case, has caused distinct differences in the offspring. 'Little Ben' is the smaller of the two (*neriiflorum* × *repens*) and has flowers of blazing scarlet. 'Little Bert' is a hybrid between R. *repens* and the taller form of R. *neriiflorum* which has been given specific rank as R. *euchaites*. Its flowers are more crimson than scarlet and while still dwarf, it is taller in growth than the almost prostrate 'Little Ben'. Both plants flower while still small, 'Little Bert' being so prolific that the foliage is hidden.

Another class of useful and pretty hybrids for the smaller garden are those with R. *williamsianum* for one parent. R. *williamsianum* itself, is a charming dwarf rhododendron with almost circular bronzy leaves and large, pink, widely funnel-shaped flowers. Unfortunately it is not hardy enough for any gardens except those on the seaboard and in warmer places inland. It is a true Category C rhododendron. Some of its offspring, toughened by hybridization are Category B—as hardy as 'Pink Pearl' and 'Britannia'—needing only wind-shelter, and some shade in southern and eastern gardens. In the West, shade does not seem so vitally necessary, although most rhododendrons are better for it.

'Humming Bird', although rated in Category C in the *Rhododendron Handbook* and in spite of having the slightly tender blood-red R. *haematodes* for its second parent seems reasonably hardy. I know gardens where it has withstood zero frosts in winter without serious harm. The May frosts that damage the new growth are a more serious danger. 'Humming Bird' is a fine little rhododendron with red stalks and pleasing rounded leaves of dark green which have some of the brown indumentum of R. *haematodes* on the underside. It flowers freely in April with large, drooping rosy-crimson bells which fade to vermilion shaded pink. 'Humming Bird' makes a mounded bush eventually four feet high and as much through.

'Bowbells' is rated hardier (Category B) and is very attractive with bronzy R. *williamsianum* foliage and wide, shell-pink bells with deeper shading on the outside, carried in loose trusses in late May. Its other parent is the fine old coral-pink 'Corona'.

There is a newer hybrid 'Jock' (Category B—*williamsianum*× *griersonianum*) which is a most attractive plant and which must be hardier than its parentage would lead one to expect. This is said to have R. *williamsianum* foliage with deep pink bells and, as one might imagine, the introduction of R. *griersonianum* blood is said to have lent a hint of orange to the flowers.

'Temple Belle', with the lovely R. *orbiculare* for its other parent, is tender, but suitable for sheltered or coastal gardens. It favours R. *orbiculare* with tubby, bell-shaped flowers of Persian rose, and makes a typical neat, rounded bush.

'Dormouse' is another good pink ('Dawn's Delight'× R. *williamsianum*). Unfortunately, it also is tender and must be kept to more favoured gardens.

Yellow rhododendrons have a special charm, and 'Cowslip' (*wardii*× *williamsianum*) is a reasonably hardy (Category B) dwarf which makes a neat, small bush with widely campanulate flowers of pale primrose. It flowers in April or early May.

'Nereid' (*neriiflorum*× *dichroanthum*) is another dwarf which I find pleasing. It bears pendulous bell-shaped waxy flowers of a gentle salmon-pink in May.

Later flowering red rhododendrons are particularly useful in the small garden to provide a splash of positive colour at a time when many of the softer toned shrubs are in bloom. 'Arthur Osborne' (Category B) is a dwarf which blooms in late June and has rich ruby trumpets which the *Rhododendron Handbook* describes as dark scarlet. Even later, in July, 'Redcap' (*didymum*× *eriogynum*) comes into flower and makes a low, compact bush. It is very free-flowering and dark blood-red in colour.

For mild, seaboard gardens in the South-west and West where the influence of the Gulf Stream is felt there is an unbeatable June-flowering rhododendron which makes a large, low, sprawling bush. This is the superb scarlet 'Tally Ho', with wide trumpet flowers that are the scarlet of a huntsman's coat. If I could grow no other rhododendron but this, I think I should be content, but as I said earlier it is too tender for any but the most favoured gardens.

In the Conway Valley, given optimum woodland conditions, it has survived zero in a frost-bottom so, where conditions are right, it might be worth trying in similar situations elsewhere.

The larger growers among the old hardy hybrids occupy too much space for the small gardens of today. Some of the more moderate growers which are good enough to be included in modern gardens are 'Susan' (bluest of the large-flowered rhododendrons and May flowering); 'Britannia' (crimson-scarlet—June); 'Countess of Athlone' (a pretty mauve-pink that is effective in woodland or to lighten any gloomy corner—May); 'Goldsworth Yellow' (apricot fading to primrose—May); 'Goldsworth Orange' (June), and 'Corona' (coral pink—May). Where conditions are good for rhododendrons—that is, where there is some shade, moist, well-drained woodsy or peaty soil and wind-shelter—some of the very best rhododendrons may be grown. Among those of moderate size are the May-flowering group: 'Naomi' ('Aurora'× R. fortunei) with scented, large open flowers of pink shaded with lavender and green; 'Carita' ('Naomi'× campylocarpum) with primrose-yellow flowers with a touch of pink at the petal-edge and pretty, oval, deep green, glossy foliage; 'Sussex Bonfire' (haematodes× 'Cornish Cross', rather tender) an outstanding brilliant red which makes a mounded bush about four feet high; the older 'Earl of Athlone' with glowing blood-red flowers; 'Unique' buff-apricot fading to cream; 'Lady Bessborough' (campylocarpum elatum× discolor) of which the clone 'Roberte', with salmon-pink flowers changing to yellow, is one of the most charming; 'May Day' (griersonianum× haematodes) with apple-green foliage and brilliant scarlet flowers; and the taller but excellent 'China' (fortunei× wightii) with handsome, large foliage and huge buff-yellow flowers.

In the late May-blooming group are the many forms of 'Fabia' (dichroanthum× griersonianum) of which I find most pleasing the terracotta 'Roman Pottery' which has more of the milky-orange of R. dichroanthum in its make-up than have any of the others. 'Tower Court' is useful where space is limited. It is a true dwarf, seldom more than three feet high and most free with its trusses of soft salmon-pink flowers. 'Goblin' is another R. griersonianum hybrid with 'Break of Day' for the other parent. Both scarlet and soft pink forms are available. 'Grosclaude' (*haematodes* × *eriogynum*) is a fine scarlet with tubular flowers and fine foliage with brown indumentum on its underside. 'Jacques' (*dichroanthum* × 'Day Dream') is pretty apricot which should become popular when it is more widely known.

To these may be added as they become available some of the hybrids bred at the Royal Horticultural Society's gardens, Wisley, with the object of combining hardiness with better form and colour than that possessed by the older hardy hybrids. Several good plants have already emerged from these crosses, outstanding being the red 'Beefeater' for which the late Mr. Francis Hangar, the Curator, was honoured by the Society. 'Moonshine Bright' ('Adrian Koster' × *litiense*) which it is believed may prove the hardiest yellow rhododendron in cultivation; the medium-growing, deep red 'Billy Budd', and the many forms of 'Lascaux' in yellow, tangerine, orange, and salmon-pink, are particularly exciting new plants introduced from Wisley. Equally good, and suitable for the smallest garden are the hybrids between the neat, low-growing, ultra-hardy R. *yakushimanum* and some of the older hybrids. Known as the R. *yakushimanum* hybrids we may expect shortly to see them in commerce when they will provide a wise choice for the owner of any more-exposed, small shrub garden.

I dealt with the evergreen azaleas earlier in this book (Chapter 2). There remain several groups of deciduous azaleas which are very useful in the small shrub garden. Probably the best known of these are the *Azalea mollis* hybrids, usually seen as a blare of flame which is showy enough but can be made more pleasing by the addition of yellow varieties in a 3:2 proportion (three yellow to two flame). Good varieties for the purpose are 'Christopher Wren' ('Goldball') (orange-yellow); 'W.E. Gumbleton' (nankeen); 'Comte de Quincey' (creamy-yellow), and 'Anthony Koster' (deep yellow). All of these look well underplanted with forget-me-nots which are left to seed from year to year.

Among the *A. mollis* hybrids, there are some pink-flowered varieties which mix well with the yellows but which should be kept well away from the flames unless separated from them by yellows in an all-colour group. 'Comte de Gomer', 'F. de Konick', and 'Consul Pecher' are all good, while 'Babeuff' is bright salmon-pink with an orange ray.

Fine though the mollis azaleas are when well grown (annual mulching is essential and they should not be too deeply planted and should have nothing but peat above the root-ball) there is no effect that they can create which the slightly later Knap Hill and Exbury hybrids cannot beat.

This new race of mixed-parentage azaleas has everything—a wide colour range, vigour, good scent, and fine foliage which colours brilliantly in autumn. Of the Exbury hybrids, 'Berry Rose' (rose-pink); 'Beaulieu' (pink shaded orange); 'Hotspur' (orange-red); 'Klondyke' (golden-orange); and 'Cecile' (salmon-orange) are fine. More subtle colourings may be found in some of the Knap Hill hybrids. 'Buzzard', in pale straw-yellow and pink gives a delightful apricot effect; there is the pale yellow 'Harvest Moon'; the regrettably named 'Persil' which is a delightful white with a yellow blotch; and 'Pink Delight' which is pink with a yellow eye. Other good ones are 'Lapwing' (creamy-yellow tinted pink); 'Mazurka' (coral-apricot); 'Bullfinch' (rose-red); 'Goldcrest' (yellow and red); and 'Sunset' (orange flame suffused with pink and red). They should be grouped in the same way as the mollis hybrids.

The Ghent group flowers even later than the Knap Hill hybrids and in the main consists of tall-growing plants with smaller, honeysuckle-shaped flowers. Single bushes strategically placed give a not too heavy splash of brilliant colour in the garden and are especially useful for interspersing between evergreens whereas a mixed group will make a brilliant and flowery effect in the late May or early June sunshine. 'Unique' (orange and yellow); 'Coccinea Speciosa' (startling flame-red); 'Nancy Waterer' (golden); 'Pallas' (red with an orange blotch); 'Bouquet de Flore' (bright pink and yellow); and 'Sang de Gentbrugge' (blood-red and very late to bloom) are all first-rate hybrids. Also good and long lasting are the double-flowered, very fragrant pale pink 'Raphael de Smet', deep rose 'Norma', and the yellow 'Narcissiflora'.

Some of the azalea species are useful in gardens where there is wind-shelter, light shade, and not too heavy frosts. A. vaseyi flowers in May with delicate pink, butterfly flowers on a slender, twiggy bush. Even more striking is the bright rose *A. albrechtii* with flowers of a similar type. Both make lightly built bushes of three to four feet high. They are of a different quality from the hybrids and should be planted away from them. They combine well with the woodland effect of silver birch and cherry rather than with more formal plantings.

Flowering in late June or July when brilliant shrub colour is scarce is the hardier American azalea, *A. prunifolium* with unusually large flowers of vivid orange-scarlet. This species makes a strong bush about eight feet high, but it is so good, so easy to grow, and so valuable for late colour that it should be included wherever room can be found for it. Softer in colour is *A. amagianum*, a Japanese species which needs wind-shelter. The leaves of *A. amagianum* look evergreen but are in fact deciduous. *A. amagianum* flowers at the same time as *A. prunifolium* but takes less room and its flowers though not quite so numerous are of a soft and lovely orange. Quieter in effect but worth a place in a shady corner where its blooms will be long lasting and its scent a haunting surprise is *A. viscosum* either in its typical milky-white form or in that of the pink flowered *A. viscosum rhodanthe*.

Note: After writing the paragraphs on chlorosis on page 63, I treated all chlorotic plants with magnesium sulphate (Epsom salts) at the rate of one tablespoonful to two gallons of water. All responded well. The effect of the solution is, of course, to make the ground acid, thereby tackling the trouble at source. The Murphy Sequestrene compound should render additional treatment unnecessary but I have found that any plants which remain obstinately chlorotic will often be improved by the Epsom Salts treatment.

9

Shrub Roses

In any garden of limited space it is those shrubs which have the longest season of bloom that yield the best return. Outstanding among these are the dwarf evergreen azaleas, camellias, ornamental quinces, ceanothuses, hydrangeas, fuchsias, *Daphne mezereum* and the *Daphne* 'Somerset', and those shrub roses which have two or more flushes of bloom.

Many of the forms and hybrids of the rugosa roses make large bushes, measuring five or six feet high and through, yet I think room must be found for them even in the smallest shrub garden. Not only have they a long season of flower—varieties in our garden usually bloom in three main bursts, at the end of May, in July, and again in September with sporadic flowering in between and on until the end of October—but their handsome dark green, deeply veined foliage and mounded shape makes them a valuable part of the garden framework. To these attributes must be added those of scent, an autumn colouring of ripened corn, and in certain varieties a bounty of bright, tomato-shaped hips. One may perhaps have only room for two or three rugosa varieties but they are too good to miss out and should be planted where they will not be crowded by other shrubs but will have room to grow freely and assume their pleasing characteristic shape with well-clothed branches sweeping to the ground.

My own favourite is 'Blanc Double de Coubert', a semi-double, paper-white rose, the shapely, often pink flushed buds of which open to flat, gold bossed blooms with a particularly sweet scent. 'Belle Poitevine' is a soft, mallow-pink counterpart of 'Blanc

Double de Coubert'. Unfortunately neither of these varieties bears many hips.

For free-fruiting qualities we must look to the single-flowered kinds—*Rosa rugosa* 'Rubra' with crimson-purple flowers enhanced by cream stamens and *R. r.* 'Alba' in which the orange-red hips of the earlier flowers mingle satisfyingly with the later crop of white flowers, provided that one does not dead head the earlier blooms. 'Frau Dagmar Hastrop' is one of the loveliest of all single roses, with deep pink buds opening to clear pink, wide, flat flowers, charmingly centred by cream coloured stamens.

One of the best-known rugosa roses is 'Roseraie de l'Hay' with resplendent crimson-purple flowers that Mr. Graham Thomas, the recognized authority on old roses and author of that enchanting book *The Old Shrub Roses* has likened to small paeonies. I cannot better his description.

The rugosa roses have been crossed with hybrid tea roses and others. Some of the resultant hybrids are delightful and retain the excellent rugosa habit of growth, making shapely, well-furnished bushes. Others are not so good, being gaunt in habit and more sporadic in bloom. Among the best are 'Sarah Van Fleet' with cream stamened, cupped flowers of silvery-pink and an erect but bushy habit of growth; 'Schneezwerg' ('Snow Dwarf') with clustered semi-double white blooms with golden stamen which if left unsnipped yield small but pretty orange-red hips to accompany the later blooms; and 'Pink Grootendorst'. This rose is delightful, bearing large clusters of fringed pink, dianthus-like blooms. Regrettably it has no scent but for all that it is worth growing for its unusual charm and for the airy and flowery picture it makes in the shrub border. Mr. Graham Thomas warns that this is 'not always a healthy plant'. In my part of the country—North Wales and the North-west—it does well, old bushes going on from year to year in increasing vigour. I would say, however, that this is the only rugosa that I have to spray for mildew ('Karathane' dealing with the trouble quite effectively), so in the hotter and drier south the similar but older and reputedly stronger 'Fimbriata' might be a wiser choice. 'Fimbriata' is not as perpetual in flower, its bloom being concentrated into two major bursts in early summer and in autumn.

Rugosa roses need little pruning. All that is necessary being to remove from the base the oldest wood if the bushes become too crowded, or to prune away any dead shoots.

The China roses are quite different in character. They make light, twiggy bushes which may be from three to five feet in height according to variety. They have a very long period of bloom. From the end of May until Christmas some of them are always in flower. We have 'Fellemberg' and the old 'Blush China' in a most inhospitable position on the windswept west wall of a garden shed and even there we have flowers as late as February.

For garden display and freedom of flowering 'Fellemberg' is among the best even of such a race as the China roses which are renowned for just these qualities. Unrestricted it will make a lightly built bush of five feet after three years in good soil and a sheltered position. Its froth of cherry-crimson cupped blooms are best seen against grey or mouse coloured stone. Against a white-washed wall or in the border the colour may seem a little startling. By a happy accident one of our two bushes is sited just behind the grey-leafed *Cistus skanbergii*, and the handsome sage-grey leaves of the cistus tone down the colour of the rose with good effect. In colder gardens lavender might replace the cistus.

Generally speaking, however, the China roses are not the roses for cold gardens, they need sunny, sheltered conditions with good soil if they are to give of their best. Under such conditions 'Fellemberg' will reach eight feet. It can however be sheared back to make a three-foot shrub.

Another strong-grower which needs if anything even warmer conditions than the rest of the group, with good air-drainage so that it will not succumb to frost is *Rosa chinensis* 'Mutabilis' ('Tipo Ideale') the chameleon-like forerunner of the present-day floribunda 'Masquerade'. *R. c.* 'Mutabilis', however, is much more charming than 'Masquerade' and has none of the latter's brash crudity. Its pointed flame coloured buds open to soft chamois-yellow, fade to a gentle pink, and finally turn to a mellow crimson.

Against a wall or shed, the old 'Blush China', the common 'monthly' rose will reach eight feet; in the open it is more often three to four. It bears, very freely, clusters of soft warm pink roses which have a delightful scent.

Of course there are other China roses. 'Comtesse du Cayla', 'Laurette Messimy', and 'Mme Eugène Résal' are well known but they are more suitable as bedding-roses, being less vigorous and thinner of growth. 'Fellemberg', *R. c.* 'Mutabilis', and the old 'Blush China' are true shrub roses; generous in floraison and pleasing in growth, they deserve the warmest, sunniest corner that your garden has to offer.

Moderate pruning suits the China roses best, spurring back in February to a strong bud and removing dead or weak wood.

Similar in habit and garden effect are the hybrid musks. They, too, should be pruned back in February for the best results, having the side-shoots cut back to three buds and all overlong basal-shoots being cut back by as much as a third. Needless to say all dead and poor wood should always be cut out, care being taken to prune to a bud and not to leave snags to die-back.

Musk rose hybrids are particularly free of their scent and to that very real garden asset they add a charm of bloom and softness of colouring that is altogether delightful.

'Buff Beauty', the coppery-pink 'Cornelia', and the creamy-pink 'Penelope' associate well together with small, shapely blooms carried very freely in large clusters. 'Pax' is a larger flowered white. 'Felicia' is of rather a different type. With individual blooms that are very double and of a clear silver-pink it makes a compact and floriferous bush. It is a rose to grow as an individual. 'Vanity', too, is an individualist, bearing almost single blooms of bright pink. Open and angular in habit, 'Vanity' is best when planted in groups of three or four when it will make a sturdy thicket of growth.

All the hybrid musks are so good that it is invidious to mention only a few. 'Francesca', 'Thisbe', 'Daybreak', and 'Danae' are all charming yellows whose only fault—if it is a fault—lies in their fading to ivory and cream. 'Moonlight' is a lovely white, with mahogany stems and dark green leaves, and in rich soil may be used as a climber of moderate height. Indeed, if I like any of the hybrid musk roses less than the others, it is those of stronger tones. The dark scarlet of 'Hamburg', the crimson of 'Wilhelm' and the more strident tones of 'Will Scarlet' and of the light magenta-crimson 'Nur Mahal' do not to me seem to fit in with the rest of the group, and are somewhat difficult to place in the shrub garden, isolated bushes giving a spotty effect. However the softer toned 'Magenta' with its 'old' lilac-mauve colouring seems acceptable and right. This, however, is a personal preference. The hybrid musks as a group are among the most perpetual-flowering and satisfactory of all shrub roses. They are roses which really take their place as garden shrubs. I do not think that any small shrub garden should be without them.

The Bourbons, hybrids of the China roses and the 'old' roses inherit the vigour and perpetual-blooming qualities of the former, often with the flower-characteristics of the latter. They bring an authentic 'old rose' flavour to the garden. Heavy enough in growth to stand alone in the shrub border they offer also a few moderate-growing climbers for the walls of house or garage. Perhaps the freest flowering of all is the sweetly fragrant, almost thornless 'Zéphirine Drouhin' the loosely formed, raspberry-pink flowers of which are nearer the China parent. 'Mme Isaac Pereire', on the other hand, has typically old-fashioned flowers, large and cupped, with quartered blooms packed with rolled petals and with a magnificent scent. Classified as madder-crimson, the flowers 'blue' to a pleasantly subdued shade. Although this rose is not a true climber it makes such a tall and rather top-heavy bush that it is really best grown against a wall or given the support of a tripod of stakes. It is certainly too good a rose to miss although to eyes un-accustomed to the older roses its colouring may at first seem unsympathetic. Old roses grow on one, though, and certainly they fit better into the shrub garden than the clarion colours and angular growth of some of the hybrid teas and floribundas.

A rose which is best trained as a climber is the striped 'Variegata di Bologna' with globular white flowers trigly striped with carmine which fades to purple.

An alternative to wall or pillar training with these very vigorous roses is the pegging down of the long growths in a circle so that they form large mounded bushes.

It should be emphasized here that whereas 'Zéphirine Drouhin' and its sport the slightly less vigorous 'Kathleen Harrop' (with pale pink petals that are carmine on the reverse borne on a bush reaching to only five feet) are seldom without flowers from late May until October at least, 'Mme Isaac Pereire' and 'Variegata di Bologna' flower in two main bursts, summer and autumn, with only occasional blooms in between.

Smaller and more easily managed bushes are the May- to October-flowering 'La Reine Victoria' with cupped, rose-pink flowers of an exquisite shape, and its sport 'Mme Pierre Oger'—favourite of our grandparents' day—with similarly shaped flowers in a pale creamy-pink deepening to a warmer colour in the sun.

To these may be added 'Louise Odier' with lilac-pink flowers and the same sweet scent.

As a group the Bourbon roses should be pruned in February, having old, crossing, and thin twiggy wood removed and the longer shoots shortened by a third of their length.

Some gardeners like to grow vigorous hybrid tea roses such as 'Shot Silk' and 'Peace' in the shrub border along with strong-growing floribundas of the 'Frensham' type but I do not think they look really at home in such a situation. Far better, to my mind to grow some of the specially bred modern shrub roses of which the most pleasing to date are perhaps 'First Choice' with clusters of single butterfly blooms in orange-scarlet borne on a five-foot freely growing bush; 'Morning Stars' makes a three-foot bush bearing cupped lemon-white, golden stamened blooms against dark glossy leaves, creating a pleasant moonlit effect in the border. The well-known 'Nevada', though delightful with its huge, semi-single, creamy blooms, is really too big for the small garden, as is the pink 'Poulsen's Park Rose'. Shrub roses which I have not seen but which seem to promise well are 'Golden Wings' and the single pink 'Erfurt'.

Shrub roses do best in a good, loamy soil, slightly acid or neutral. Compost and bone-meal should be dug in at planting-time and the bottom spit should be well broken up. A generous amount of peat should be incorporated in heavy soils to prevent waterlogging.

Most shrub roses are propagated by budding. If planted with the union at least three inches below ground suckers will not be troublesome and the plants will eventually become established upon their own roots.

Owners of slightly larger gardens may decide that the charm of the older roses is sufficient to justify their including those with only one season of bloom, judging them, therefore, on the same basis as other flowering shrubs. This will lead them to explore the delights of the albas, centifolias with their delightful mossed varieties some of which flower twice (in the summer and autumn), the gallicas, and damasks—all the true 'old roses' of historic times.

Some of these old roses may be used to make fragrant and decorative hedges within the garden. The striped gallica 'Rosa Mundi' which dates back to the sixteenth century or earlier has been used with tremendous effect at Kiftsgate Court in Gloucestershire where it makes a hedge about three feet high and through. The sweet-scented alba 'Maiden's Blush' is another ancient rose that is well suited to the same purpose. It makes a taller barrier. The gallica 'Charles de Mills', 'Tuscany Superb', and *R. gallica officinalis* are all suitable subjects. They should be planted two feet apart and sheared over in February when without any further support than that of their own growth they will form sturdy, compact, and very free-flowering hedges. These old roses have, of course, only one season of flower—usually at midsummer when they will remain in bloom for two or three weeks—as long as most other flowering hedging-subjects but not perhaps long enough for those of us who like our roses in bloom over most of the summer. The freest flowering rose hedge of all may be provided by the old 'Blush China' planted eighteen inches apart and similarly clipped.

Taller, self-supporting hedges may be made with the long-blooming hybrid musks 'Felicia', 'Moonlight', and 'Prosperity' or the even longer flowering rugosa 'Sarah van Fleet'.

Some people like a screen of rambler roses trained upon wires. Such roses should be planted about ten feet apart in well-dug ground generously supplied with guano or fish-manure. They will require rather more attention than the self-supporting roses suggested earlier, the old canes being removed from the base each September when the season's new growth should be tied in their place. For the shrub garden some of the ubiquitous and more brazen modern varieties such as 'Dorothy Perkins' and 'American Pillar' are best avoided. In their place I would suggest the creamy-yellow and very fragrant 'Goldfinch' interplanted with the wine-purple 'Rose-Marie Viaud' or 'Purple East'. Or one might choose some of the *R. sempervirens* ramblers which have the advantage of being almost evergreen. The large-flowered 'Flora', whose exquisite centifolia-like flowers are of a warm lilac-pink, might be inter-planted with the pale blush 'Adelaide d'Orleans' or that pretty cottage favourite—the white flowered 'Félicité et Perpétue'. All these flower only once a year, at midsummer. The Bourbon 'Zéphirine Drouhin' may be similarly trained and will yield its sweet, raspberry-pink blooms sporadically—and in my experience, prolifically—after its first June floraison until October. Cheap offers of 'wonder' rose hedges should be treated with suspicion. These usually turn out to be nothing more or less than budding briars, *R. canina*, the wild rose of the hedges and completely unsuitable for the purpose advertised.

Although one feels that in the really small garden those roses with several flushes of bloom are the best value, there are one or two groups and individuals which are so rewarding that they should be planted wherever room can be found for them just as one would plant a prunus or a philadelphus in spite of its single flowering season and because one feels that single spell of bloom is too good to miss. On such grounds one must include the May-flowering group of yellow roses. One of the very best of these, a *R. spinosissima* hybrid from Germany, 'Frühlingsgold'—whose few-petalled blooms are of a clear yellow that does indeed seem the very colour of spring—is unfortunately a big sprawling shrub (8 × 8); the bright gold 'Canary Bird' (6 × 6) from Korea is another vigorous grower but it does not thrive everywhere. North Wales is one of the places where it does well, perhaps like the really old roses—the albas, gallicas, damasks, and centifolias—

it appreciates a moist soil and a humid atmosphere. It is a superb rose with large, single flowers of a deep butter-yellow (the colour of butter from Jersey milk) enhanced by amber stamens. Those who feel they cannot afford the space for either of these may like to try 'Harison's Yellow'—*R.* × *harisonii* (this spelling is correct) (5 × 3)—with a sparse, erect habit and semi-double, sulphur-yellow flowers that are very freely borne. *R. primula*—the 'incense rose'—reminds one of a potentilla with its many primrose-yellow, single flowers that are no bigger than a sixpenny-bit. It deserves a place, where space can be found in the small shrub garden, for the attractive blooms no less than for the incense-like fragrance that arises from its leaves on warm, damp days.

Many new shrub roses have been bred but not all have the right effect for shrub garden use. Among those which best fit in are the single pink perpetual flowering 'Ballerina', the single 'Lilac Charm', 'Marguerite Hilling', a pink flowered sport of Nevada but smaller growing, and the trailing 'Raübritter' with cup-shaped double pink flowers. This last flowers for about seven weeks in July and August and is ideal to trail over a low wall bounding a terrace or to use in a similar position in a more formal part of the garden near the house.

Shrub roses are particularly useful to bridge the gap between the main flush of flowering shrubs in spring and the hydrangeas of late summer.

Shrubs for Spring

Of all the shrubs seen in spring gardens the forsythias are probably the best known and loved. *Forsythia × intermedia* 'Spectabilis' (8 × 6) is the one we see most often of all but this makes a vigorous bush which may become almost unmanageable in a small border. It may be restrained by pruning immediately after flowering and by cutting out superfluous shoots from the base but it is such a strong-grower that pruning is troublesome and to my mind *F. suspensa* (5 × 4 if pruned as advised) is easier to manage in spite of its trailing shoots. Trained to a short leg with its stems cascading freely it is a pretty sight in the border, weeping above a low-growing rhododendron or behind a dwarf Japanese quince, the orange-scarlet of which will make a striking contrast with the lemon-yellow of the forsythia. It must, however, always be cut back severely after flowering—to within a bud or two of the old wood is not too much. If this is neglected the bush will become a mass of tangled shoots with the flowers borne only at their ends while the centre of the bush is bare of bloom. *F. suspensa atrocaulis* is a variety with purple stems which show off the flowers most effectively. It needs the same treatment as the type.

Many people would not agree with me, but I find the softer yellow flowers of the *F. suspensa* varieties much more pleasing than the brazen harshness of the *F. intermedia* 'Spectabilis' gold.

F. i. 'Lynwood' (6 × 5) is quite a strong-growing variety, as is *F. i.* 'Arnold Giant'. Neither have the grace of *F. suspensa* and the flower colour of both is crude. *F. i.* 'Arnold Dwarf' errs at the other extreme with pale washy colouring and is not at all free-flowering. Where a really small forsythia is needed, for the front row of a border or for rock-work, the American *F. viridissima* 'Bronxensis' (1×2) is a better shrub.

Very early flowering is the Korean *F. ovata* (4×4), which is a compact grower and undoubtedly the best forsythia for the really small border. Its graceful, primrose-yellow flowers associate well with *Rhododendron* × *praecox* (5×4) which often blooms at the same time.

Yellow is, I suppose, the dominant colour in the spring garden, but in no other genus does it express the spirit of the season as charmingly as in the corylopsis family. There is something about the soft yellow, cowslip-scented flowers, hanging like catkins from the bare branches in March and April that calls to mind Easter chicks and skipping lambs, daffodils, primroses, and all the other Easter joys.

Corylopsis pauciflora (4×5) is perhaps the most charming. It makes an extremely free-flowering, densely branched bush of up to four feet but its flowers are susceptible to frost and where it cannot be given a sheltered position, the tougher *C. spicata* (8×8) would be the better choice. It is a slightly taller grower than *C. pauciflora* but not so tall as *C. willmottiae* (12×10) which makes an elegant shrub with greeny-yellow, very fragrant flowers in long drooping racemes. None of the corylopsis are fussy as to soil but they do need as sheltered a position as you can give them, with a backing of evergreens or hardy deciduous shrubs to protect them from the prevailing wind. An evergreen backing is best, where it can be contrived, because it will help to show off the pretty yellow of the corylopsis catkins. With this genus, particular attention should be paid to watering during hot summers otherwise the next season's show of flowers will be poor.

Even earlier to flower, usually in February, is *Stachyurus praecox* (5×3), a quietly distinctive, reddish barked shrub which bears its long-lasting, creamy bells in curiously stiff, finger-length ropes which do not move in the wind.

With the stachyurus, *Daphne mezereum* (2×3) is usually in bloom with its sweet-scented, starry, rose-purple flowerlets in clustered heads. Its white variety *D. m.* 'Alba' is lovely and its creamy flowers are followed by yellow berries. Both are easily increased from seed sown when ripe and should be more often planted. Daphnes take up so little garden room and yet they are so rewarding with their long flowering periods and wonderful scent.

D. mezereum is very hardy. It does not dislike lime and thrives best in a stiff loam in semi-shade. The deeply cultivated soil of old cottage gardens suits it and no doubt it benefits from the diet of tea-leaves and soapy water which the country-folk bestow on it. I often copy them and pour the contents of the tea-pot, when cold, over any cherished or ailing plant. Several invalids have recovered under this treatment and daphnes and lilies thrive. But to return to more orthodox methods . . . all the daphnes appreciate flat stones placed over their roots to keep them cool and to retain the moisture.

D. × *dauphinii (hybrida)* (3 × 3) is an early spring flowerer that begins to open its buds in winter. It is a hybrid between the later *D. collina* and the tender, winter-blooming *D. odora* which should be grown against a wall. *D.* × *dauphinii* needs no such coddling except in the bleakest gardens. Evergreen like its parents, it bears sweetly fragrant, rosy flowers.

Quite different, semi-prostrate in habit, is *D. blagayana*—a coveted gem which starts to flower in February. *D. blagayana* (1 × 3) sends out long, sprawling branches which should be anchored to the ground by having stones placed over them. They will then root as they go and the shrublet will spread. A well-grown plant of this variety may be a yard across and bear sixty or seventy terminal clusters of richly scented, creamy starlets. It likes a cool, leafy loam, and the stone-layering I have described is essential to its well-being.

D. cneorum (1 × 2), the garland flower, is of similar but less sprawling growth, and it too appreciates stone-layering. It flowers much later than *D. blagayana*, in May, and is one of the prettiest of the daphnes with small, sage-green leaves and heads of rose-pink flowers. Like all the family it is fragrant. All daphnes and especially *D. blagayana* and *D. cneorum* should receive a top-dressing of peat or leaf-mould after they have flowered. Such a top-dressing usually results in the side-shoots throwing out roots. Some of them may then be detached to form new plants against the inevitable and unpredictable demise of the parents.

Berberis darwinii (8×6) is a well-known but first-rate shrub which flowers at the same time as *Forsythia suspensa*. It has tiny, holly-like, evergreen leaves and drooping clusters of orange bells which are brilliant in the spring sunshine. In our garden this berberis is planted between *F. suspensa* and *Amelanchier canadensis* (10×8) the Snowy Mespilus. The amelanchier makes a slender tree with airy sprays of white flowers and prettily tinted young foliage which burns with particular fire in autumn. It does not bloom for as long a period as the forsythia and berberis so an addition to the group could be made by planting *Viburnum carlesii* in front.

The most brilliantly flowered berberis is *Berberis linearifolia* (6×4) with shapely leaves and rich orange-red flowers. There is a hybrid between *linearifolia* and *darwinii* known as *B.×lologensis* (6×4) which is beautiful with its clusters of bloomy apricot flowers.

For the smaller border there is *B.×stenophylla* 'Irwinii' (3×3) like a miniature *B.×stenophylla*, which makes a compact bush seldom more than three feet high with small, needle-like leaves. Good varieties are *B.×s.* 'Coccinea' with crimson buds opening to little coral coloured bells, *B.×s.* 'Corallina' with coral buds opening yellow, and *B.×s.* 'Corallina Compacta' which is even smaller.

There is also a useful, low-growing form of *B. darwinii* known as *B. d.* 'Prostrata', but here the orange bells of the type are orange only in the bud, becoming golden-yellow as they open.

Old favourites in most gardens are the ornamental quinces which used to be known as cydonia but which should really be called chaenomeles (pronounced kee-no-meeles; keeno for short). They are valuable for their apple-blossom-shaped flowers in spring and golden, quince-like fruits in autumn. They may be grown against a wall where their blooming will be both earlier and more prolonged, but they are grand border shrubs and look well overhanging a pond or stream. For the small border the low-growing *Chaenomeles speciosa* 'Simonii' is best.

C. × superba 'Rowallane' (4 × 8) makes a vigorous spreading bush and is very floriferous with bowls of scarlet-flame. Another chaenomeles of similar habit is 'Knap Hill Scarlet'. 'Boule de Feu' (5 × 6) is softer in colour, more of an apricot-flame. We have this variety in our garden and find it vigorous and free-flowering. Either 'Rowallane' or 'Boule de Feu' looks well grouped with the snowy *C. s.* 'Snow' (6 × 6) which, by the way, is the variety—with the apple-blossom *C. s.* 'Moerloosii'—to use against a red brick wall where the flame and crimson varieties might clash. *C. s.* 'Cardinalis' (*umbilicata*) (8 × 8) is a good salmon-pink form, and there is the soft flame 'Phyllis Moore', semi-double and a very good plant to train against a wall. 'Boule de Feu', also, is easily trained as is the newer blood-red 'Ely Mossel'. In the open it is possible to keep these *C. speciosa* varieties to three or four feet in height so that they form much-branched, attractively spreading bushes for the front or middle of the border. All chaenomeles should be winter-pruned, spurring back to a flower-bud as one might prune an apple tree. This vigorous cutting back not only keeps them within bounds but greatly encourages blossom production.

I wrote about the dwarf Russian almond—*Prunus tenella* 'Fire Hill Form' in an earlier chapter but there is a shrubby cherry also which is effective in the border. This is *P. incisa* (6 × 5), the Fuji cherry. The type blooms in March with white flowers and rosy buds which seem to cast a warm glow over the bush. *P. i.* 'February Pink' is an earlier form with pink flowers and there is also a winter-flowering variety *P. i.* 'Praecox'.

Among the loveliest shrubs in spring are the tree heaths which are so useful, even when out of flowers, for their pleasant mounds of dark or mossy green. *Erica arborea* 'Alpina' is one of the hardiest. Its average height is about six feet but the bush may be kept lower if clipped over after flowering. Like the more tender *E. arborea* it will stand a slightly alkaline soil. *E. mediterranea* may also be used.

E. australis (6 × 4), the rosy-lilac, southern heath from Spain, and its white variety 'Mr. Robert', are more tender. In well-drained stony soils in full sun they will withstand average winters in many gardens.

Another lovely tree heath which is not fully hardy (it will stand twenty degrees of frost) is *E. lusitanica* (7 × 6) (*codonodes*). *E. lusitanica* is of the *E. arborea* type but rose-red in bud and the style and stamens of the opened bells are a rich pink. This seems to cast a pink flush over its moss-green fur when the bush is in flower. It has the longest blooming period of all the heaths, opening its first few flowers in November and increasing in floraison in every mild spell until spring when the whole bush will be covered with little pink-tinged bells. This heath increases by self-sown seedlings and it is worth watching its outer skirts for their appearance. *E. × veitchii* (7 × 6) is a hybrid of *E. lusitanica* and is supposedly hardier. It has the same rosy-flush in bloom and gives off a pleasant fragrance but it has a shorter flowering season, opening its bells all together in spring. A danger to these last two heaths in our garden was that our cats loved their fragrance. They rubbed against them and sometimes caused damage. A wise precaution where cats are kept would be to wire-net the first two feet of growth when the plants are young.

Towards the end of April the first of the brooms, *Cytisus × praecox* opens its sulphur pea flowers. At the same time a less hardy broom, the Porlock broom—*C.* 'Porlock' (4 × 4)—a hybrid between *monspessulanus* and *racemosus*, will begin to open its racemes of golden flowers on a warm wall or hot, dry bank, or it may begin to flower earlier, particularly if planted against the breasting of a frequently used chimney. We grew, too, against a south wall *C. racemosus* (4 × 4) (*Genista fragrans* of greenhouses). This is a delight with its golden racemes of flowers like those of a small laburnum, but it is advisable to keep replacement-cuttings under glass during the winter in case the parent plant is lost by hard frost.

On chalky or limed soil *Spirea arguta* (6 × 6), the bridal wreath, is valuable at this season, making a shapely deciduous bush up to seven feet. It is very pretty when massed with its tiny white flowers and may easily be kept to a size suitable to restricted areas, by pruning after flowering.

Among the commoner shrubs which I would never despise are the ribes or flowering currants. These are pretty so long as no attempt is made to clip them into forced shape.

The pale pinks seem usually to flower earlier than the deeper colours. *Ribes atrosanguineum* (8×8), 'Edward VII', and 'Pulborough Scarlet' are all good red forms but I would always keep a bush of the old flesh-pink for early flowers.

If cut early in January and allowed to open in a warm room the flower-racemes will be white and, with the bright emerald of the unfolding leaves, some branches will be pretty and effective in a vase.

In our present garden *Viburnum* $\times$ *bodnantense* 'Dawn', which begins to flower in late October, continues in bloom until March and is thus one of the most valuable long-season performers, especially as its foliage is bronze when young and takes on a similar warm shade in the autumn, blending with that of its neighbour *Rosa rubrifolia* and providing obliging branches to act as hosts to purple and pink flowered clematis 'Jackmannii Superba' and 'Hagley Hybrid'. It makes an appealing picture. I have described this present garden in detail in my book *The Very Small Garden* in which readers may find further developments of the colour theme.

II

Shrubs for May and June

At this time the lime-free garden has vivid colour masses to draw upon from the rhododendron and azalea families. To soften and supplement these, or—for alkaline soils—to replace them, the brooms are valuable.

Two genera of allied shrubs go under the common name of broom. These are the genista (genista is the badge of the Plantagenets from which the Royal House took its name) and the cytisus. Cytisuses thrive on most soils except pure chalk on which the genistas will be a better investment. Liking sunny, well-drained places with full exposure, the brooms are subject to wind-rock and will be helped by a heavy boulder placed over their roots to anchor them. To make compact, sturdy bushes they should be sheared over after flowering. Exceptions to this rule are the taller *Genista aetnensis*—*G. cinerea*, and *G. virgata* which should be trained to a stem and allowed to cascade downward as described earlier.

Taking the cytisus first, there are two early May-flowering hybrids of considerable garden value. Both are low growing. *Cytisus beanii* has a profusion of golden-yellow flowers sheeting its foot-high mound, while *C. × kewensis* has creamy flowers that remind one of the April-flowering *C. × praecox*. Neither of these are seen at their best on flat ground. They are superb cascading down a bank or may be planted behind a boulder and allowed to weep forward. *C. × kewensis* is sometimes a slow starter, making one or two long shoots at the expense of bushier growth. To cure this the longer shoots should be trimmed back after flowering to within a bud or

91

two of the old wood. Strong side growth will then result in the desirable waterfall habit that one associates with well grown specimens of this broom. C. *purpureus* (2×4) is an interesting dwarf with rosy-purple or pink flowers which contrast pleasantly with the creamy-yellow of C.×*kewensis*, while C. *hirsutus* (2×2) is a sturdy but rather sparse little shrub, usually up to two feet with hairy young shoots and yellow flowers marked with brown. It flowers from late April or May until August and in sheltered places may flower even earlier.

A little later in the month the lovely white Portugal broom, C. *multiflorus* (6×4) is in flower. This is a tall grower which may well be used, trained to a tall leg and staked, to supply light shade to some of the rhododendrons that flower at the same time. It would look well with the pink, green-shaded rhododendron 'Naomi' or the lilac-mauve 'Countess of Athlone', or would make a cool and attractive group with the blue 'Susan' and the yellow 'Dairymaid'.

Still later the many *Cytisus scoparius* hybrids and varieties flower. Most of them are appealing with their soft and charming colour combinations. However, some of the pink and crimson bi-colours do not show up well in a glade planting where distant colour effect is necessary. Here the moonlight broom—C. *s. sulphureus*—is good, with its mass of pale lemon flowers which its name so aptly describes. This is a useful variety to associate with blue flowered rhododendrons or, on alkaline soil, with the evergreen ceanothuses. Another broom with clear colour effect is 'Cornish Cream' the creamy buds of which open into flowers with deep yellow wings and cream coloured standards. 'Goldfinch' is delightful with fawny pink, scarlet, and yellow flowers which give a soft apricot effect as gentle as the colouring of a cock chaffinch's breast.

'Fromow's Purple' makes a rosy-purple colour splash that is effective with the golden broom of the moorlands, while 'Mrs Norman Henry' is a graceful lavender-pink.

Of the genistas, *Genista lydia* (2×3) flowers in late May and sometimes until the end of June. It is a splendid little shrub up to two feet in height with clear yellow flowers covering its strongly arching branches which roll inwards in a distinctly uncommon and not unpleasing manner. This genista needs a warm, raised, well-drained position so that its wood ripens well and is able to withstand the frost. *G. pilosa* 'Nana' ($1\frac{1}{4} \times 3$) is another dwarf, making a mass of twiggy shoots about eighteen inches high and carpeting a wide area with its golden flowers. Like *lydia* it does best in a dry, sunny part of the garden and is excellent for covering a bank or the raised front of a bed.

The coronillas bear a family resemblance to the brooms with their golden pea-like flowers. They have soft green pinnate leaves. *Coronilla glauca* (6×4) is a fine shrub for a hot, sunny position on a bank or against a warm wall. It is evergreen and seldom out of flower. Its continual floriage makes it a notable winter-blooming subject. It is tender, however, and will only succeed in a position such as I have described. Much hardier, but deciduous and usually flowering only in summer *C. emerus* (8×4) is a pretty shrub with similar, rather smaller, yellow pea flowers tipped with sienna. This is a scandent shrub which will scramble happily up a wall or bank or may be used to decorate a dull evergreen.

Lovers of sunny, well-drained places, the evergreen ceanothuses associate well with the brooms and coronillas. All of these are unfortunately on the border-line of hardiness, but given a sunny, stony, well-drained soil or a warm wall they will stand most winters in all but the coldest gardens. They are so pretty with their bright blue, thimble-shaped flower-heads that they are worth trying in any suitable situation. They are liable to wind-rock and so succeed better if large stones are placed over the roots to anchor them. Oddly enough, although they must have good drainage if they are not to succumb to winter cold and damp, these ceanothuses will not withstand too long a period of drought without watering and during the exceptionally dry summer of 1959 many well-established bushes died.

Ceanothus veitchianus (7×6), one of the best known, is also one of the most tender. Except in the mildest counties it needs the shelter of a wall.

Ceanothus 'A.T. Johnson' (6×5) has flowers of bright blue and it blooms not only in the spring but again in the autumn as does 'Delight' (6×5) with its long panicles of deep blue flowers. 'Delight' is a very hardy hybrid.

Lavender and rosemary are useful shrubs for sunny places and the grey foliage of one and the greyish green of the other make them useful as contrast plants. *Lavandula spica*, the old English lavender, will make bushes of two to three feet which should be sheared over after flowering. There is a lilac-pink variety which may be used to add interest, and also the dwarf deep purple 'Hidcote' which makes a good plant for the front of the shrub border while *L. s.* 'Nana Alba' is a very small, sweet-scented, white flowered variety.

For hot dry places where *Coronilla glauca* thrives, it is worth trying the distinctive *Lavendula stoechas* (1×2) from the *maquis* with its dark purple, square flower-heads topped by bright blue-purple cockades.

There are several good forms of rosemary in addition to the usual *Rosmarinus officinalis* (6×5) which will make vast bushes, man-high, in any sunny place with the necessary well-drained soil. It stands clipping well and can easily be kept within bounds. In dry, sunny places it may be used to form a pleasantly aromatic hedge. *R. lavandulaceus* (1×3) is a useful mat-forming plant, ideal to clothe a boulder or to sprawl across paving. It is more tender than the common rosemary and must have full sun to ripen its wood and sharply drained soil to help it to withstand frost. It often begins to flower in March or even earlier. Most of the really bright blue-flowered rosemarys are tender and need the protection of a wall. 'Tuscan Blue' in particular suffers from this drawback. There is, however, a hardy variety which makes a low, compact plant and has flowers of brilliant blue. This variety is known as 'Severn Sea' (2×2).

In this country the rosemarys seldom attain the full brilliance of flower such as is seen in their native habitats of Corsica, Capri, and Majorca. There the brightness of flower colouring seems to be due to some content of the volcanic soil in which they grow. In Britain one may achieve a similar end by watering the soil around the bushes in November and spring with a quarter of a teaspoonful of ammonia dissolved in a bucketful of water.

The leptospermums are attractive, sun-loving shrubs from New Zealand which unfortunately are hardy only in the milder districts of the British Isles near the western and south-western seaboards. Elsewhere they need to be against a wall. However, it is only frost which harms them; they do not seem to mind wind. Double varieties of leptospermum have recently been introduced into commerce but somehow doubling seems wrong in plants which belong so essentially to the open spaces of the wild, and I do not think one need look beyond the colourful single species of which the well-known *Leptospermum scoparium* 'Nichollsii' (7×5) with its crimson blooms and the larger flowered pink variety *L. scoparium* 'Splendens' (7×5) are two of the best. *L. s.* 'Chapmanii' (7×5) is another very free-flowering bright pink. These leptospermums will often have a second period of bloom in November.

However, the leptospermums, desirable though they are, must remain shrubs for the lucky few with suitably mild gardens. *Buddleia alternifolia* (8×8), on the other hand, is a shrub for everyone. It is, moreover, a shrub of distinction and charm which far surpasses that of its later summer-flowering relations of the *B. davidii* class. *B. alternifolia* is a gentle, graceful shrub with long arching stems which are wreathed in early summer with delicate lilac, sweet-smelling flowers. It should never be cut back in spring in the manner so frequently recommended for *B. davidii* and its varieties as such pruning would spoil its habit and result in loss of flowering. If it becomes too large for its allotted space the offending stems should be removed from the base. Occasionally the oldest stems may be removed in the same way. There is a good hybrid between *B. alternifolia* and the tender *B. caryopteridifolia* which is known as *B. × pikei* 'Hever' and is very hardy. To the charm of *B. alternifolia* is added, in *B. × pikei* 'Hever', stronger flower colour in the two-foot-long arching spikes of tiny lavender-pink flowerlets. The leaves, too, are attractive with a covering of woolly-white indumentum.

Totally different is the orange buddleia—*B. globosa* (8×6)—which some people dislike but which I find pleasing with its sunny globes of orange-gold. These ball-like inflorescences are made up of many tiny flowers. They glow among the dark green leaves, giving this wind-resistant, fairly hardy shrub a character entirely its own.

Another early summer shrub is *Choisya ternata*, the Mexican Orange Blossom which is especially valuable in the lime-ridden garden to replace the evergreen mounds of the rhododendrons which will not grow there. Usually it flowers for a second time in September and it appreciates a sheltered, wind-free site.

Quite indifferent as to soil and wind, and completely hardy, the weigelas (diervillas) (5 × 5) are pleasant enough with their foxglove like flowers. Their growth is attractive if the branches are allowed to arch naturally and if pruning is restricted to cutting out old wood from the base instead of the bush being mutilated to the shape of clipped privet as one sometimes sees. The red flowered weigelas seem to me dull and dark in colour and to make little show at a distance. The pink varieties—*Weigela rosea*, 'Abel Carrière', 'Conquête', and 'Le Printemps', and the pretty creamy-white, pink flushed 'La Perle' add more to the garden scene.

Deutzias (4 × 5), are another genus of easily pleased shrubs which are especially useful on account of their ability to flower in quite dense shade. They do best if the old flowering wood is removed immediately after they have bloomed. *Deutzia campanulata* is very hardy and makes an upright-growing bush of about five feet with white flowers which are large for the genus. *D. vilmoriniana* is attractive with its broad clusters of snowy flowers. For those who prefer coloured blooms there are *D. rosea*, *D. grandiflora*, *D. elegantissima*, *D. kalmiaeflora* and the hybrid 'Magician', the last three of which are shrubs of the highest quality with beautifully shaped, clear-cut flowers of delightful lilac-pink, borne on gracefully arching sprays. This is a family of pretty shrubs which ask only a little wind-shelter and are hardy and accommodating, resisting drought and cold alike and flowering generously every year.

The kalmias are a rhododendron-like genus which do best in moist, lime-free soil in full sun. They bear trusses of unusual saucer-shaped flowers in shades of pink and red which cover the rhododendron-leafed bushes in May or June giving an effect like

1. A Japanese azalea, colourful and compact for the small garden

2. *Carpenteria californica* is not fully hardy but can be a delightful addition if given a warm, sunny corner backed by a wall

3. *Cercis siliquastrum*, the Judas Tree, with its crop of rosy-mauve flowers

4. *Cistus* 'Silver Pink' is not fully hardy in all districts but does best on a sunny bank

5. *Clematis tangutica obtusiuscula*—its seed-heads are as decorative as its yellow flowers

6. *Clethra alnifolia* 'Rosea', the Sweet Pepper, a fragrant August-flowering shrub

7. *Cytisus battandieri* is a delightfully fragrant member of the broom family from Morocco. It is distinguished by its silky foliage, chunky golden heads of flower, and pineapple scent

8. *Daphne cneorum* 'Variegatum' is the variegated form of the pretty, rosy-flowered, rock garden daphne. Like all daphnes, it resents disturbance and should be given a sunny spot with a stone over its roots to retain moisture

an old-fashioned cotton print and so giving rise to the American name of 'Calico Bush'.

Kalmia angustifolia 'Rubra' (3×3) is one of the most striking. It is usually seen as a three-foot bush and carries deep red flowers in June. The type *K. angustifolia* is similar but in this the flowers are rosy. *K. glauca* ($1\frac{1}{2} \times 3$) is a small wiry shrub—a foot or two high, with narrow bright green leaves which are glaucous beneath and heads of vivid rose-purple flowers in early May. *K. latifolia* (5×4) is a bigger shrub, ultimately five or six feet high. It is pleasing with its glossy leaves and large heads of deep pink flowers in June, and is a good shrub to plant by a pool or stream as it loves moisture. *K. l.* 'Myrtifolia' is a dwarfer form with narrower leaves and large pale rose flowers. It makes a neat mounded shrub which looks well among heaths or dwarf azaleas.

Many shrubs which are often regarded as tender, like the ceanothuses and the Tuscan rosemary, prove reasonably hardy when grown in full sun in well-drained soil preferably on a bank of raised soil. Such are the cistuses—the lovely rock roses of Southern France and the Mediterranean with their silky, crumpled saucers of bloom which fall at noon in the *maquis* but often last until evening under our more cloudy skies. Fallen, they lie beneath the evergreen bushes like broken butterflies.

Many of the cistuses have large and splendid flowers but it is one of the quieter ones that I like best—*Cistus × skanbergii* (3×3), a hybrid, with sage-grey leaves and inch-wide dog rose blooms of gentle pink. *C. × skanbergii* will grow to a height of about three feet. I have seen it used as a low hedge on a dry bank in Anglesey, and it is quite hardy with us in North Wales. Given the conditions I have described it will withstand most winters in many places and I firmly believe it to be hardier than the vaunted 'Silver Pink'. *C. × corbariensis* (2×3) also has small flowers, white this time, and is probably the hardiest of all the cistuses. It makes a low, spreading bush of two to three feet. Much larger are the white saucer-like blooms of *C. ladaniferus* (6×6)—the gum cistus—with their showy maroon central blotch. *C. cyprius* (6×6) is hardier than the aromatic *C. ladaniferus*. Like *C. ladaniferus* it grows to six or eight feet and makes a vigorous bush with narrow dark green leaves and three-inch white saucers with a broad crimson blotch. *C. × purpureus* (5 × 5) is another vigorous grower with vivid rosy-crimson flowers. It is similar to the smaller growing *C. villosus* 'Sunset' (4 × 3) with magenta-rose flowers that to some eyes may seem somewhat garish but which may be softened if the shrub is grown against a greyish sun-baked stone. An excellent small cistus is the handsome leafed *C. crispus* (1 × 2) with yellow eyed flowers of brilliant magenta-pink. The cistuses as a whole are a most desirable genus, showy enough for the pageant of June, providing useful green or grey hummocks of foliage in winter, and obliging enough to grow in chalky or lime-ridden soils.

Escallonias do not mind alkaline soil. Their only limitation is the fact that they are not sufficiently hardy for bleak northern districts. *Escallonia macrantha* (7 × 5), the evergreen hedging shrub, will not be killed in winter in more exposed Midland districts, but it will lose its leaves. In the Midlands, if you wish your escallonias to be truly evergreen, they should have the shelter of a wall. Throughout the southern counties I believe the escallonias prove fairly hardy with the exception of the beautiful, white flowered *E. × iveyi* (6 × 5) and *E. organensis* (a shrub of which I have no personal knowledge but which is famed for its lustrous leaves and large pink flowers).

E. edinensis (4 × 4) makes a neat four-foot bush for the small garden where it is more easily controlled than the vigorous *E. macrantha*. It has smaller leaves and pretty rose-pink flowers. 'Slieve Donard' (7 × 6) is attractive, too, with its large panicles of apple-blossom pink, while 'Donard Brilliance' (6 × 6) is a shrub of particularly graceful habit with arching branches and large rose-red flowers.

The potentillas are a charming genus of moderate-sized shrubs with pretty pinnate leaves and small, wild-rose-shaped flowers of various shades of yellow or cream. They are deciduous, very hardy, with an ability to thrive in sun or shade and to adapt themselves to any soil, that should win them a place in every garden. Most of them begin to flower in May and June and continue until September. *Potentilla fruticosa* 'Buttercup' makes a moderate-sized shrub (3 × 2) with leaves made up of three or five leaflets and inch-wide, golden-yellow flowers. 'Katherine Dykes' is similar but taller growing (5×5) and is very floriferous with primrose flowers. .P. 'Vilmoriniana' (5×3) is attractive—a moonlit shrub with silver-white leaves and pale primrose flowers. P. *mandshurica* (2×2) makes a pleasing shrub, low and spreading, with pure white flowers borne on purple stems above its mats of grey foliage.

Lupinus arboreus—the tree lupin—is useful for hot dry places or to fill in gaps until the more permanent shrubs have grown. Its fresh green foliage lasts through the winter and, provided the bush is sheared over after flowering, it makes a shapely mound (4×6). Its scented spikes of white, yellow or purple are carried freely throughout the early summer.

With their scented breath, the mock oranges—philadelphuses— are redolent of midsummer. The dwarf, double 'Manteau d'Hermine' and the dainty three-foot *Philadelphus microphyllus* (shy-flowering at first in northern gardens) are ideal for the front of a border, or in a very small garden they may be grown as sole representative of the genus. Two taller doubles—excellent as back- or middle-row plants—are the well-known 'Virginale' (7×7), and 'Albâtre' (6×4), which to my eye is prettier.

Philadelphus 'Belle Etoile' has huge square flowers with purple staining at the centre setting off the golden stamens and is first rate. 'Sybille' is another purple stained variety with arching branches and an enjoyable scent.

Other white flowered early summer shrubs whose main charm lies in the distinction and arrangement of their flowers are the viburnums. *Viburnum opulus* 'Sterile' (8×8), the double guelder rose, is a strong, back-row shrub with big white 'snowball' flower-heads. The 'Japanese snowball'—*V. plicatum* (6×6) is even better. Both of these are shrubs of fascinating but artificial appearance. They belong to the formal garden rather than the more informal. Suitable for either is *V. p.* 'Mariesii' with its white, lace-cap flowers and horizontal branches and velvety green leaves. The flowers are freely carried all along the branches so that an established bush in flower is a wonderful sight. An added attraction of this viburnum is its outstanding autumn colour, the leaves turning a deep wine red. It is usually seen as a four-foot, wide-spreading bush. Smaller is *V. p.* 'Rowallane' which succeeds it in flowering-time. This variety has slightly smaller flower-heads which are more dome-like in shape. *V. macrocephalum*—the 'Chinese snow-ball' has over-large clumsy heads of flowers and is not as hardy as the Japanese varieties.

Like the mock oranges, the viburnums grow happily in either alkaline or acid soil.

The early flowering yellow shrub roses such as 'Canary Bird' and ✕ *cantabrigiensis* come into bloom in mid-May and should be considered in building up colour pictures within the garden. They associate well with the summer flowering viburnums.

A June-flowering white spiraea, *S. nipponica* 'Rotundifolia', is useful to accompany pink Rugosa roses such as the beautiful single 'Frau Dagmar Hastrop'.

Good to associate with white or soft mallow cistus on a sunny bank, the Moroccan broom, *Cytisus battandieri* is one of the delights of our present garden with its silky, laburnum-shaped foliage and chunky cone-clusters of pineapple-scented golden flowers.

12

Late Summer Bloom

Standbys of the July and August garden, the hydrangeas are yet not so widely planted as they might be. It is thought, perhaps, that they are tender shrubs that thrive only by the sea-side. In fact they will flourish in many inland gardens. We grew them successfully in one of the bleakest districts of North Staffordshire. Given well-drained but moist soil and good frost drainage they will do well in many Midland and northern districts. In frost-pockets or -hollows they may be grown in large pots, sunk into the soil for the summer, and in winter given the protection of a greenhouse or spare room. Failing this, in such a situation grow the ultra-hardy *Hydrangea paniculata* (6×6) with its handsome greenish heads which change to white and become pink as they age.

The lacecap hydrangeas are the most artistically satisfying of the garden varieties. They are, however, plants for some shade—not for the full sun where the mop-heads will thrive.

Hydrangea colouring puzzles many people. The fact is that most hydrangeas are naturally blue or white because they grow in nature in an acid soil. In an alkaline medium the natural colouring becomes distorted to pink or red, which may be quite pleasing none the less. On mildly acid soils hydrangeas often need the help of a 'blueing' agent if they are to achieve a good blue colour quickly. It is unwise to apply such an agent in the plants' first season. In the second autumn spread aluminium sulphate (one pound for a three-stemmed plant and proportionately upwards) in a circle over the roots and leave it to be washed in by the weather. Alternatively one may treat the plants with Sequestrene

It is impossible to blue a white hydrangea; all one can do is to enhance the blue of the eye and thus to bring out its full beauty. Some large hydrangea bushes may need blueing treatment for two or three seasons before they become really blue. This treatment also benefits the foliage of the plant and turns the leaves a rich green. On chalk, or in limed soils, hydrangeas often have sickly yellow leaves. These may be helped by the same treatment or by spraying the foliage with Sequestrene which contains chelated iron plus manganese and other elements which are specially beneficial to hydrangeas. On excessively alkaline soils it is impossible to turn the flowers blue and so plant-associations should be worked out that are in keeping with the pink and red colour schemes. For instance pale pink hydrangeas would look well with white roses and the blue plumbago-flowered *Ceratostigma wilmottianum* or the feathery blue *Caryopteris* ✕ *clandonensis*, the 'blue spiraea'.

Of the mop-headed hydrangeas, the magnificent 'Altona' and 'Hamburg', whose large, serrated florets and huge flower-heads turn to vivid red in autumn, are only for the maritime counties. Inland, such varieties as 'Vibraye', 'Mousseline', 'Parsifal', and 'Westfalen' will prove more satisfactory. 'Westfalen' is a fine red. In acid soil it turns violet and does not blue well. 'Mme Moullière' is a wonderful white. 'Vibraye', 'Mousseline', 'Holstein', 'Hamburg', and 'Altona' are all good blues when grown in acid soil. 'Maréchal Foch' is a good dark blue while 'Vulcan' (2×2) is a very dwarf red which becomes deep blue when treated or in acid soil.

Tidy gardeners should resist the temptation to cut off the dead flower-heads in autumn. These should be left to protect the young shoots from frost. Hydrangeas should never be cut back. The only permissible pruning is the cutting out of surplus shoots from the base of old bushes if they become overcrowded.

Hydrangeas need a moisture-retaining soil which, however, must not become waterlogged. A heavy loam is ideal or they will thrive on the bank of a stream or pond. Where such luxuries are not available the site must be made as congenial as possible for them by the incorporation of peat into the soil. Slabs of stone over the surface of the soil above the roots will also help and a mulch of green bracken in June, applied when the ground is really wet after rain or thorough watering will help to conserve the moisture in the soil and will also increase the intensity of flower colour. Copious watering during dry spells is essential.

Brooms such as *Genista cinerea* and *G. aetnensis* are useful to associate with blue hydrangeas. *G. virgata* (8×6) from Madeira is attractive also and has silky foliaged shoots to add to its charm. It blooms too early to coincide with the hydrangeas but is effective to associate with the old blue-mauve *Rhododendron* 'Fastuosum Flore Pleno' in June.

Spartium junceum (8×6) is a tall broom-like shrub with narcissi-scented, daffodil-yellow flowers in late summer. It thrives in a hot, well-drained position and has the advantage of an extremely long-flowering season. It blooms until late November in our district.

Quite different in character are the hypericums with golden, bowl-shaped blooms. *Hypericum calycinum*, which is often called the 'Rose of Sharon', is a dangerous pest in small gardens on account of its invasiveness and the difficulty of eradicating its creeping stems. Its place may be taken by the large-flowered *H.* × *moserianum* (2×3) which, although supposed to be slightly tender and, I believe, cut by frost in Surrey, thrives in Derbyshire, or by the taller hardy *H. forrestii* (3×3) which has the additional advantage of fine autumn colour. 'Hidcote' (4×3) is a fine hypericum but it is not hardy enough for the bleakest gardens. In good soil, in semi-shade it makes a fine mounded bush which if sheared over in March will become studded all over with flowers. Even better is 'Rowallane' (5×3) but this is definitely a plant for the milder counties or to be grown against a wall in colder places. Against a wall in good soil it may in time reach eight feet high or more. All these hypericums have a long season of bloom often beginning in June and continuing to the end of October. So attractive and so valuable in the late summer garden are they that they should be found a place in every border. Quite hard pruning should be practised each March if the best show of flowers is to result.

As with many supposedly tender shrubs the less hardy hypericums prove tougher and more frost-resistant when grown either against a wall or in full sun with sharp drainage. In milder places they will grow and flower well in half-shade.

Buddleias (8 × 6), sometimes called 'butterfly bushes', are popular with many gardeners and they are pleasant enough with their arching wands of scented mauve, purple, white, or lilac flowers which always seem to attract the red admirals in July and August. Better than the varieties of *Buddleia davidii* is *B. fallowiana*, and its variety *Buddleia fallowiana* 'Alba', with pleasing white-woolly foliage and slender, more graceful spikes of lavender or white flowers.

Fuchsias are good summer and autumn shrubs and there are several hardy varieties which, although they may be cut back by frost in the winter, will sprout strongly again the following spring. They should, of course, be grown against a south wall in cold districts and should always be planted in poor soil with sharp drainage to prevent their making sappy tender growth. Apart from the well-known *Fuchsia* 'Riccartonii' (4 × 4) there is the pretty, ghost-pale *F. magellanica* 'Alba' (3 × 4), the large-flowered 'Mrs Popple' (4 × 3) with red and blue-purple flowers, and 'Mme Cornellison' (4 × 3) with elegant red-and-white pendants.

Flowering more often in September than in August, the hibiscus (8 × 3) is a hardy deciduous shrub for a well-drained, sunny place. It is rather late in coming into leaf and its foliage is perhaps coarse but its wide, showy trumpets make it a desirable occupant of garden space. One or two dwarf shrubs planted in front of it will draw the eye away from its gauntness before the flowers arrive. Good varieties of *Hibiscus syriacus* are the rosy-crimson 'Woodbridge', white *H. s.* 'Totus Albus', and lavender 'Bleu Coeleste'. Finer still, with larger and more splendid trumpets, is the newly introduced *H. sino-syriacus* which is equally hardy. The varieties of this species so far available are white with vivid central blotches.

Because the tamarisks are often seen at the sea-side they are sometimes suspected of being unsuitable for inland planting. Actually this genus will do well in most inland gardens provided the soil is not too shallow or chalky. Tamarisks should be planted in full sun. Although they grow well in sandy sea-side soils, inland they do best in good, medium loam. They are grand for windswept gardens but it should be remembered that although they look like evergreens they are in fact deciduous and so cannot be called upon to form part of the permanent garden structure. Plant them behind a medium-growing evergreen such as choisya, and their feathery foliage and plumes of flower will be a summer delight. *Tamarix pentandra* (8× 5) is the species to choose for late summer bloom. When in flower the whole bush seems to be wreathed in rose-pink smoke. *T. p.* 'Rubra' is less subtle but more showy with rosy-red flowers.

Another shrub often seen at the sea-side is *Senecio greyi* whose value lies in its rounded hump of handsome grey foliage. The yellow daisy flowers which appear throughout the summer are sunny but ordinary. Some people cut them off. We leave them because they look sunny and do not detract from the value of the senecio as a foliage shrub. It is reasonably hardy inland except in the bleakest places.

When one thinks of yellow one invariably thinks of the complementary blue and there is a good July/August blue flowered shrub in *Ceanothus× burkwoodii* (5× 5) with its shiny, oval evergreen leaves of about an inch long and bright thimble-like panicles of flowers up to two inches long. The *Ceanothus* 'Autumnal Blue' (6× 5) is similar but the flowers are of a softer blue. Both bloom in May as well.

Several deciduous ceanothuses bloom at this time. I do not think they are such good shrubs for garden effect as the evergreen kinds although their flowers' panicles are larger. They are, however, hardy in most gardens, particularly in sunny, sharply drained soil. One of the most reliable is 'Gloire de Versailles' (6× 6) with smoky panicles of pale blue flowers. It makes a rambling shrub up to ten feet high in sheltered places but may easily be kept low. Large old bushes are certainly eye-catching and of considerable value in the late summer garden. I would plant the golden *Spartium junceum* near by for a shrub grouping which is satisfying over a long period. 'Henri Desfosse' is a brighter blue ceanothus, while 'Ceres' and 'Georges Simon' have flowers of pinkish-mauve, and pink, respectively.

Cytisus nigricans is a six-foot broom with spire-like racemes of yellow flowers in July and August. It is useful to plant in front of the ceanothuses 'Gloire de Versailles' and 'Henri Desfosse' for additional contrast, and also to give winter form to the group, although it is not as long-flowering as *Spartium junceum*.

An ally of the brooms, *Indigofera gerardiana* (5 × 3) is a pretty shrub for July. It has pleasing pinnate leaves borne on gracefully arching shoots, and sprays of pinky-purple pea flowers. While not being one of the showiest garden shrubs it is distinctive and holds the eye with its charm. *I. hebepetala* is even more pleasing, when obtainable, with crimson-and-rose coloured flowers, and there is an attractive dwarf Chinese species known as *I. decora* with racemes of pink and white flowers.

The hebes which used to be known as veronicas are among the most useful shrubs for windy sea-side gardens. As evergreens the members are valuable garden furnishings throughout the year while their bottle-brush spikes of tiny, funnel-shaped flowers are quietly pleasing and in some *speciosa* varieties showy. *Hebe speciosa* (5 × 5), with the brilliant purple *H. s.* 'Alicia Amherst', red 'Redruth', and bright pink *H. s.* 'Gloriosa', are shrubs for the maritime counties. Hardy throughout the south is the violet 'Autumn Glory', the dwarf mauve, 'Bowles Hybrid', lavender 'Midsummer Beauty', and *H. brachysiphon* which is sometimes listed as *H. traversii*.

Desfontainea spinosa (4 × 4) will grow in Perthshire, but it is more at home in milder climates where in lime-free soil it is an interesting and worth-while plant. Rather like a holly, the desfontainea is one of those 'catch-question' plants with which gardeners of the old school enjoyed trapping the unwary. A certain clue to identification lies in the positioning of the leaves on the stem. In the desfontainea the leaves are opposite, while in the holly they alternate. In late summer the desfontainea puts on a show of dangling, yellow tipped, crimson-apricot trumpets which I find fascinating. Here in North Wales it is hardy. In colder counties away from the Gulf Stream influence it should be grown against a west wall. It strikes easily from half-ripe cuttings taken in July and rooted in a closed frame. It dislikes being too dry at the root and prefers shade for part of the day. It is this question of positioning which sometimes prevents plants from doing their best.

Romneya coulteri (5 × 5), the Californian tree poppy, likes a south wall where its succession of great, silken, white poppy flowers with golden centres will burst upon an admiring world from July until October. It may be increased by careful removal of the running underground stems in spring. *Romneya trichocalyx* is very similar but does not increase so rapidly by underground stems. Both may be propagated by means of root-cuttings as described in Chapter 22.

The clethras are a treasured race of sweetly scented late summer-flowering shrubs. All have long racemes or panicles of white flowers. *Clethra delavayi* (10 × 6) will eventually grow to ten feet high and is striking with its six-inch racemes of black anthered, half-inch wide, milk-white flowers with pretty, scalloped edges. *C. fargesii* (8 × 6) has longer but more slender racemes and flowers after *C. delavayi* in August. *C. barbinervis* (6 × 5) carries on into autumn with less showy but very graceful long racemes. All need a lime-free soil. The three mentioned above are fairly hardy in North Wales but for most districts the well-known *C. alnifolia* (6 × 5), the 'sweet pepper bush' is a safer choice along with its variety *C. a.* 'Rosea' in which the flowers are tinged with pink.

Hoheria lyallii (6 × 10) is a beautiful shrub with fragrant white cherry-blossom blooms and downy, grey leaves that give it a translucent, underwater quality. Coming from New Zealand the hoherias do best against a wall in the colder counties. *H. lyallii* is a spreading shrub but it is so appealing that it well deserves its garden space.

Spiraea bumalda (3 × 4) is a useful shrub for the front of a border and has flat heads of warm rose-red flower; its variety 'Anthony Waterer' is a fine crimson.

A bush or, in mild districts, a small tree which will always catch one's attention is the Chilean *Tricuspidaria lanceolata* with neat, dark evergreen leaves and large crimson bells which glow from the dark branches like hanging lanterns giving it the appearance of some giant fuchsia. Near the sea in North Wales *T.*

lanceolata is hardy in the open but in many districts it will need the protection of a wall—a north wall will do. In fact it prefers a shady position. It propagates easily. A flat stone placed over a low-growing branch to anchor it to the ground will result in the production of roots or it may be struck from half-ripe cuttings placed in a shaded frame in July and planted out the following spring.

In late July and August the rugosa roses will be embarking on a second spate of heavy bloom. Towards the end of August and into September their flowers will be mingled with a show of their large, scarlet, tomato-shaped fruit. At this stage the contrast of the white flowers of 'Alba' with its extra large fruit and the smaller white 'Schneezwerg' with its very bright hips is particularly attractive.

13

Autumn Colour

Although one thinks of autumn in terms of leaf colour and berried fruits there are several shrubs still in flower, the beauty of which should be taken into account when planning the autumn garden.

Of these *Spartium junceum*, the ceanothus 'Gloire de Versailles', hibiscuses, hypericums, hydrangeas (whose flower-heads will soon turn green and crimson with age), caryopteris, and romneya are among the best. Many of the hebes are true autumnal flowerers. Seedlings of the willow-leafed *Hebe salicifolia* (4× 5) (wall shelter inland) in our garden regularly come into bloom in September, October, and even later, while the *H. speciosa* hybrids bloom for a second time in November and December. On a windy west wall in our garden *H. s.* 'Alicia Amherst' and 'Redruth' flower until early February and give a substantial contribution to the winter garden and to the house-vases with their brilliant spikes of purple and crimson respectively.

A true shrub of the season is the evergreen ceanothus 'Autumnal Blue'. This ceanothus needs the shelter of a wall and is handsome with its small leathery leaves and blue thimbles which are larger than those of most of the evergreen members of this genus. At the same time *Lespedeza thunbergii* (*sieboldii*) (*Desmodium penduliflorum*) (7× 5) comes into bloom, its arching branches weighed down by panicles of large pea flowers. This shrub is most effective when planted where the daffodil-yellow of *Spartium junceum* can complement its rosy-purple. In cold areas, however, it may frequently be cut back by winter frost and so assume more of a herbaceous aspect.

In the small garden, autumn leaf colour is often a luxury. One cannot afford space to plant many shrubs for such colour alone. Most must be dual-purpose, adding year-round grace, or spring or summer flowers to the garden in addition to their colourful contribution to autumn's funeral pyre.

Foremost among these are the azaleas. The Ghent, mollis, and especially the Knap Hill, hybrids, colour well, as do the species, while some of the dwarfer evergreens turn to crimson and rose. The leaves of the rugosa roses colour to warm gold. *Amelanchier canadensis* is brilliant, while *Berberis thunbergii* (5×5) becomes a mound of fiery scarlet.

Of the shrubs and small trees which are grown for beauty of form rather than flower or fruit, the silver birch is pre-eminent, with a rain of golden leaves against the silver trunk. The dwarf maples colour well and both the green and purple forms of *Acer palmatum* and the cut-leaf *A. p.* 'Dissectum' add autumn fire to the interest of their summer form.

Where possible shrubs and trees for autumn colour should be grouped about the garden so that one or two composite pictures are assured. Our best group is composed of Knap Hill azaleas and the Ghent hybrid 'Raphael de Smet' in front of a common spindle tree.

Autumn and winter are the seasons when we look in addition to the beauty of bark and form and of leaf colour to the brightness of berries, to delight us in the garden scene. Too often, however, we are disappointed. Sometimes the wrong form of a tree or shrub is planted, and so no berries result. Or the berries prove too attractive to the birds and so their show passes all too quickly. The most commonly planted pyracantha for instance is *Pyracantha coccinea* 'Lalandii' (8×8) whose berries attract more bird robbers than any other. The smaller-leafed *P. rogersiana* (6×5) has a form *P. r.* 'Flava' that bears shining yellow berries which for some reason the birds ignore. This, or the dwarfer 'Knap Hill Lemon' or 'Buttercup' are the firethorns to choose.

Cotoneaster berries must be less palatable to the birds. At least they seem to be left untouched throughout the winter in my district. *Cotoneaster horizontalis* is the best cotoneaster for planting against a wall. For other purposes, the wide selection that this genus offers is not nearly as much used as it might be. Where a small tree—or even a series of small trees to form a thicket or screen—is needed the hybrid 'Cornubia' (15 × 12), with *C. frigidus* for a parent, will make a widespread mound of growth up to twenty feet high. 'Cornubia' is a well-dressed shrub, clothed with rich green leaves from the ground, but if you wish it may be pruned as a tree, leaving five or six feet of trunk clear. The great beauty of 'Cornubia' is its berries, which hang in huge bunches of brilliant red through the autumn and right into winter.

C. conspicuus is another brilliant. It lives up to the description given it by the great plant-hunter, the late Mr. F. Kingdon Ward, as being a 'bubbling cauldron of berries'. It is delightful, too, in flower when the single white hawthorn blossoms wreathe its interlacing branches, but it is the prodigality of its large scarlet berries that compels us to plant it. Two forms of this shrub are available: an upright form growing from three to six feet high, and the more prostrate *C. c.* 'Decorus' (3 × 5), which is excellent, sprawling at the front of other shrubs or curtaining a retaining wall. Good too, for the front of the shrub border, or to plant among rocks in any garden on acid soil, are the pernettyas. There are often complaints about the lack of berries with this family, but the remedy is simple. Many of the pernettyas (2 × 2— taller if unpruned) are unisexual; so to ensure free-fruiting, selected male forms should be planted to every group of females.

The Davis's hybrids are a group of large-berried seedlings with fruits as big as small marbles, coming in a variety of shades, from pinky-white through lilac and rose to mulberry. *P. mucronata* 'Alba' is one of the loveliest of the genus with large pure white berries. This is one which definitely needs the presence of a near-by male plant if it is to fruit. The Davis's hybrids are supposed to be bisexual and not to need a male, but to be sure I like to include the attractive lower growing *P. thymifolia* in every group.

Lack of berries on hollies often stems from the same cause. Some hollies, such as 'J.C. Van Tol' (8 × 5), bear both male and female flowers and so can be relied on to berry freely every year. Others, including many of the variegated forms, are male and will never berry. Good females are the misleadingly named 'Golden King' (6×5), *Ilex aquifolium* 'Argenteomarginata', and *I. a.* 'Flavescens', but to my mind one of the most appealing is the yellow berried *I. a.* 'Bacciflava' ('*Fructoluteo*'), whose fruits will add great distinction to an otherwise conventional Christmas floral arrangement.

For the really small garden where a fully grown holly might be out of place, the skimmia is an ideal plant. Bird marauders do not touch skimmia berries, which often remain on the bush until midsummer; but with this genus unisexuality is again a problem. *Skimmia japonica* 'Foremanii' however, is bisexual and will form a two- to three-foot bush with broad, gleaming foliage and bright scarlet berries.

Some of the berberis family have fine berries. One which is noted for its autumn leaf colour too, is the three-foot *Berberis wilsonae* (3×3) whose only drawback is the extreme prickliness of its many sharp spines. Its berries are rosy and have a translucent quality that reminds me of the miniature bunches of artificial fruit that one associates with Victorian glass domes. *B. aggregata* (5×4) may reach five feet but it may well be kept to a lower height. It bears large panicles of bloomy berries which in their scarlet join the conflagration of the dying leaves.

Stranvaesia davidiana salicifolia (8×5) is a vigorous, erect-growing evergreen shrub some of the leaves of which turn scarlet in autumn and winter to vie with its brilliant clusters of berries.

From scarlet berries to white. *Symphoricarpus racemosus* 'White Hedge' (3×5) is a good variety of the common snowberry that is appealing when its cold, glistening white berries are borne from October until Christmas is over, but it is a rambling, sprawling bush and is best confined to the back of a shed or some other place where one can have the enjoyment of the berries—which incidentally are good for cutting—without giving up more valuable space. There is also the newer and less rampant symphoricarpus 'Magic Berry' (3×3) with fruits of glistening carmine. This and the pink hued *S. orbiculatus* are pretty to mix with sprays of the pink flowered autumn cherry—*Prunus subhirtella* 'Autumnalis Rosea'—in vases for the house.

For acid-soiled gardens where rhododendrons thrive, the

gaultheria family offers some colourfully berried small shrubs. The gaultherias enjoy moist, peaty soil in semi-shade and are ideal to provide attractive close boskage for the front of north-facing beds. In flower they are very similar to the heaths. *Gaultheria miqueliana* ($\frac{3}{4} \times 2$) is a nine-inch-high undershrub with white berries and apple-green leaves. *G. cuneata* ($1\frac{1}{2} \times 2$) is taller with larger white berries and bright green, narrow leaves. *G. tricophylla* ($\frac{1}{4} \times 2$) is the great beauty of the family, a four-inch-high carpeter with berries as blue and as big as a hedge-sparrow's egg. *G. procumbens* ($\frac{1}{4} \times 3$) the 'partridge berry' of North America is a spreading carpeter which adds to the attraction of its bright red berries a useful faculty for keeping down the weeds. Taller growing, *G. fragrantissima* has dense clusters of navy-blue berries.

Very different is the sea buckthorn with its shaggy, silver leaves and bright orange-yellow berries. *Hippophae rhamnoides* (6×5) is a unisexual shrub so both male and female plants must be purchased.

Add to these the rounded tomato-like fruits of *Rosa rugosa*, the brilliant red jujubes of the climbing honeysuckles, the orange of the rowan and the rose-flushed white currants of its relation *Sorbus hupehensis*, and the garden in autumn will not be without its feast of colour.

An additional enchantment to twine through a hedge or cover the roof of a shed or garage, *Celastrus orbiculatus* (15×15)— relation of the spindle berries—is one of the most brilliant fruited climbers that exist. The fruits last until January—the corn-yellow capsules splitting wide to reveal the scarlet seeds. Male, female, and hermaphroditic forms of this climber exist so care should be taken to ensure that a self-fertile form is chosen.

The true spindle berries, too, are an autumn delight with their seed-capsules dangling from long stalks like coral-pink or crimson parcels. They thrive in most soils, enjoy chalk, and will stand shade. The common *Euonymus europaeus* (8×8) is one of the best, both for fruit and autumn foliage colour. *E. alatus* is good and adds the strawberry-pink of its dying leaves to the charm of its large red capsules. By cutting branches when in fruit for indoor decoration one may not only have the joy of spindle berries indoors but may keep the shrubs to a suitable size.

14

Winter Beauty

Unlike those gardens which are dependent on bedding-plants for their colour, the shrub garden has no dead season. The use of winter-flowering trees and shrubs builds up pictures whose delicate winter beauty rivals in appeal the more garish splendours of high summer.

An outstanding shrub which begins to flower in November or even October is *Viburnum farreri* (7 × 5). This viburnum is a tall, upright-growing shrub, apt to form a thicket at the base. When established it flowers very freely with small heads of rose-flushed, tubular, white flowers that have a clove-like scent. Even better with larger flowers which last longer in water is *V.* × *bodnantense* (8 × 5), a hybrid between *farreri* and *grandiflorum* with the hardiness of *V. farreri* allied to the bigger flower-clusters and rosy hue of *V. grandiflorum*. *V.* × *b*. 'Dawn' is the best clonal form of this cross. *V. farreri* flowers best in an exposed site with full sun but *V.* × *bodnantense* needs and deserves some shelter. Both benefit if some of the suckers are removed from the base to be bestowed upon lucky gardening friends.

Some people may feel they have no place suitable for the gangling six- or eight-foot-high bushes which these two viburnums may become. To them I would commend the dwarf *V. farreri* 'Nanum' (1 × 2), though it may be some time before it flowers freely. All winter-blooming viburnums need a year or two to become established before they flower freely. The green leafed pure white flowered *V. f. candidissimum* seems to flower at an earlier age than the bronzy leafed, pink-flushed form which with us took a full three years to give a reasonable return of flowers. Since then it has been more generous with its blooms each year.

Along with the winter jasmine—*Jasminum nudiflorum*—these are the main pre-Christmas flowering shrubs for the average garden. The winter jasmine is so lovely with its showers of golden stars against the bare green branches that I think it should be used more freely than it is. We grow it on four different walls, facing north, south, east, and west so that its flowering period is prolonged. It is in fact our main standby, along with *Iris unguicularis*, bergenias, *Daphne mezereum*, and twigs of witch hazel and autumn cherry to fill the vases for the house. Thoughtfully planted, a shrub garden of less than a quarter of an acre can provide flowers for the house, day-in, day-out, throughout the year.

Some people advocate pruning the winter jasmine by cutting back the side-shoots after flowering, but plants which are used for cutting as much as are ours, need no additional pruning.

In mild districts, along the south and west coasts and in other warm, sunny localities, *Rhododendron* 'Nobleanum Venustum' (7×6) will often open its pink flower-trusses in November. Where it does well *Camellia sasanqua* 'Narumi-gata' (oleifera) (5×4) makes a charming companion. Its scented blossoms are as informal and refreshing as those of a wild rose. In a warm spot it yields plenty of flowers for cutting as well as for garden decoration, but it is very susceptible to strong winds, the foliage bruising easily. I planted this camellia in part of the garden where no other plants had shown signs of wind damage, yet within a few weeks its foliage was flagging and bruised so I transferred it to the shelter of a wattle fence which situation seems to suit it well. Like most camellias 'Narumi-gata' layers easily and the mounding over of its lower branches with peaty soil before weighting with large stones will result in new vigorous young plants to increase one's stock or to exchange with friends.

Before Christmas, too, the fern-leafed *Clematis balearica* from the Balearic Isles will begin to flower against a wall. This is an elegant evergreen with finely divided, bronzy, ferny foliage and open, bell-like flowers of greenish yellow that are appealing if quiet in their charm.

WINTER BEAUTY

A shrubby member of the honeysuckle family—*Lonicera* × *purpusii* (6 × 6) will not set the Thames on fire with any blatancy of beauty. Its attraction lies in the scent of its creamy, small honeysuckle flowers which are pleasing in their poise, and though not long spurred as are the climbing members of the family, they have noticeable finish in the airy jauntiness of their prominent stamens. *L.* × *purpusii* is a hybrid between the old *fragrantissima* and *standishii*. Like them it should have a sheltered position but it enjoys the sunshine. Plants in full sun are more free-flowering than those in shade. The flowers are bigger than those of either parents but *L.* × *purpusii* is almost entirely deciduous whereas *L. fragrantissima* has the advantage of keeping most of its leaves in winter.

With us, the golden ribboned witch hazel, *Hamamelis mollis* (7 × 7) opens its brown furry buds for New Year's Day. *H. mollis* is said to like an acid soil but does well in our alkaline soil when planted in rhododendron peat. Where there is room, the orange flowered *H. m.* 'Brevipetala' might be planted close by. Together they will light the January garden. Like many winter-flowering shrubs *H. mollis* is long-blooming. The popular *H. m.* 'Pallida' has large sulphur yellow petals and a sweet delicate scent.

Daphne mezereum 'Grandiflora' (*autumnalis*) is a plant which seems to have disappeared from commerce; at least I have been trying to find a plant for years with no success. It was useful in old gardens with its habit of flowering from autumn throughout the winter. *D.* × *hybrida* is a good substitute, and the more tender but exquisitely scented *D. odora* will do well against a wall.

We find in many winters that the common *D. mezereum* (usually 3 × 3—occasionally larger) breaks into flower from November on, although this year, following a wet and sunless summer it did not bloom until February. There are several colour forms of this daphne, some with larger blossoms than others and it is worth begging ripe berries from good forms and raising your own seedlings. *D. m.* 'Alba' is likewise variable. Sometimes these daphnes unaccountably die so it is as well always to have plants of various ages coming on in different parts of the garden. Daphnes dislike moving, so plant the young seedlings from a pot into their permanent stations. Like other scented plants I think they should be grown whenever possible at the side of a path so that their fragrance may be caught as one passes by.

Country belief holds that *D. mezereum* should be planted in threes because it likes company. This is true in so far as that many plants—contrary to popular thought—do better when their roots have the companionship of others. Is this due to the aeration of the soil caused by other roots breaking down the particles, or to the larger roots drawing moisture into the area? I do not know, but I do know that many otherwise difficult plants do best in root-ridden soil.

All daphnes enjoy a cool root-run and benefit from a slab of stone placed on the soil over their roots.

Partly because a small garden and an insatiable love of plants has driven us to it my husband and I plant more closely than many gardeners think wise. By using plants of varying heights—a spreading dwarf in front of a tall-legged tree and so on—we try to give each plant room to follow its natural habit. Nevertheless, bulbs, shrubs, trees, and herbaceous carpeters all grow in close association and we find that not only do they give each other shelter and company for the roots, but grown closely they do keep down the weeds.

A good dwarf winter-flowering shrub to use as weed smother is *Sarcococca humilis* which usually grows only to twelve or eighteen inches high. It will grow in deep shade, is dense enough to keep down any weeds and has tiny white flowers—little more than stamens and stigmas—borne beneath the leaves, and a heavenly scent which brings to the greyest winter day an illusion of summer.

As a rule I am not fond of variegated shrubs with the exception perhaps of isolated specimens of gold or silver hollies. One variegated shrub, however, which is of great value in the garden during the winter months is *Elaeagnus pungens* 'Maculata' (6 × 6) whose glossy green foliage is brilliantly splashed with gold.

Mahonia japonica has everything—handsome foliage, long flower-sprays, and a wonderful lily-of-the-valley scent. It needs wind-shelter and does not mind sun or shade. For very exposed gardens it can be replaced by the admirable *M. aquifolium* (3 × 4) with its attractive pinnate leaves and short upright racemes of bright yellow flowers which are not, however, borne until spring. M. 'Moseri' is useful for the contrast of its foliage which turns to a reddish colour in winter.

In addition to these shrubs which grow well in the open garden there are several attractive winter-blooming plants which need the protection of a wall. One of the best of these is the evergreen *Coronilla glauca*. Hard frost may nip some of the blossoms but others will take their place. Plant *Lithospermum rosmarinifolium* (if you can get it) or the lithospermums 'Grace Ward' or 'Heavenly Blue' at its foot in good lime-free soil and you will have a combination of gold and blue to bring summer to your garden from November until March. This grouping is often successful on a hot dry bank, but for safety in all but the mildest counties I would grow the coronilla against a sunny wall.

Azara microphylla (10 × 6) is often listed as hardy but it is a plant which is safer against a wall except in very mild places. It is slow-growing with neat, small leaves but eventually it forms a small tree when its dainty foliage will show handsomely against a cream background. Out of flower it might be taken for a species of box but in February it bears puffs of tiny yellow flowers, larger than those of the sarcococcas but, nevertheless, humble enough to be missed by the unobservant. Few people, though, could miss their scent—a perfect vanilla fragrance—so strong that a twig is enough to scent a room; more might be overpowering.

Chimonanthus praecox (8 × 6)—the winter sweet—is a completely hardy shrub which is usually grown against a wall, probably because it is most free-flowering in such a position. It is also a shrub which takes a long time—often up to seven years—to flower, so it is not a shrub for the impatient or for those with very limited space. If you intend to stay in your present garden for life, plant the winter sweet and in later years you will bless the day you did so. With its quiet, yellow flowers and wonderful scent it will capture and enchant you. Try to get the form *C. p.* 'Grandiflorus' because this is much finer and more showy than the type. *C. p.* 'Luteus' also is good, with clear yellow flowers without the maroon staining of the type.

Abeliophyllum distichum is not fully hardy and is usually grown against a wall. It flowers at an earlier age than the winter sweet and is a shrub which is not seen nearly as often as it should be. A relation of the forsythias, it is quite different from them with its abelia-like leaves and sweetly scented white tubular flowers flushed with pink which usually open in February. It may be increased by layers, but unlike those of camellias and rhododendrons which root very easily these need certain preparation. A tongue should be cut from the underside of the branch to be layered. The cut thus made should be held open by a matchstick and inserted in the soil while the end of the layered branch should be bent into as upright a position as possible and then secured to a cane. The acute bend in the wood slows up the sap flow and so encourages the shoot to send out roots to augment its nourishment.

The Japanese quinces or chaenomeles usually begin to flower in the winter—even when grown on a north wall. Two very early varieties are the 'Aurora' and 'Lady Moore'. These, too, need patience. They take three or four years in which to establish themselves and to build up a framework before they flower freely or make very much of a show.

That is the tragedy of the modern gardener. It takes twenty years to make a garden and the exigencies and circumstances of modern life move many of us to pastures new long before that. If you have the chance to stay in one place, make the most of it and plant these long-term investments, enjoying the years of expectancy and waiting until they mature.

South of London and along the south and west coasts the mimosa—*Acacia dealbata* (20 × 12)—is a good risk on a warm wall, particularly against the chimney-breasting of a much-used room. This is so lovely, the steely blue of its feathery foliage being almost as much of an attraction as its fluffy yellow ducklings of flowers, that it is always worth trying even in the unlikeliest places. In some years it may be cut by frost but often it will come again; and what is a garden—or life for that matter—without adventure? It is gambles such as these, taken against the chances of climate, which when they come off render the enjoyment of one's garden the sweeter.

No especial difficulties should be encountered in growing *Garrya elliptica* (7×5) successfully against a north or a west wall. The male form of this shrub is the one to choose for the length of its suede-green catkins which contrast so effectively with the dark evergreen leaves. Often one can pick the catkins for Christmas and they make a distinguished decoration in a white pottery vase. In the garden the garrya looks best against a cream, or grey stone, wall.

Itea ilicifolia is a largish shrub which can be kept pruned, cutting back alternate shoots every other year so as to ensure its supply of fragrant greeny white catkins each autumn: these often last well into the winter.

The beauty of winter bark should not be forgotten and, although there is not a lot of room to spare in a small garden, space might be found for the scarlet-stemmed dogwood *Cornus alba* 'Atrosanguinea' (8×8) which with us is a rather enthusiastic grower but which does not mind being pruned back each spring to a stool. In fact this treatment encourages it to send up plenty of brightly coloured young shoots. It should be placed where the sinking sun can shine through the stems and light them up. In our present garden we have this shrub in association with the orange-tinsel *Hamamelis × intermedia* 'Jelena', yellow *H. mollis* and the rosy purple semi-deciduous *Rhododendron mucronulatum*. *Erica carnea* 'Ruby Glow' carpets the ground in front and the resultant picture does much to lighten winter gloom.

15

Carpeters and Weed Smother

There are three methods by which weeds may be kept down in the shrub garden. The first entails the application of a six-inch mulch of bracken or dead leaves over the whole area in June or autumn. Bulbs will come up through this mulch; so a garden in which this method is practised may still have its daffodils, lilies, leucojums, dog's tooth violets, and other bulbous treasures. However, the mulch would smother all herbaceous plants as well as weed growth.

The second method entails the planting of the whole shrub area solid, using a close boskage of dwarf evergreen shrubs to fill in spaces between the larger shrubs and to cover the ground at the front of the border. This gives an attractive appearance to the garden and has the advantage of remaining tidy and interesting even in the depth of winter.

But some people want to grow a few herbaceous plants—special favourites—as well as shrubs, and for them the third method is preferable. This consists in mulching immediately round all trees and shrubs—taking care to keep the mulch away from direct contact with the trunks or stems—and leaving areas for the planting of good herbaceous carpeters which, as they spread, effectively keep down the weeds in their path. This method has the drawback that some weeding is necessary in the early stages before the ground is clothed. So it is not the method for those who want only an immediate effect and have but little time to spend in their garden. For those whose gardens are their hobby and delight, it is ideal.

Several basic requirements are essential in the carpeting-plants chosen. They must be strong-growing and need little attention or pampering. They should cover the ground for most of the year and they should be pleasing, colourful, or interesting in themselves.

The various hellebores—the sculptured *Helleborus argutifolius* (*corsicus*)—which may grow up to three feet, with its nodding green heads of flowers; the handsome *H. foetidus* the specific name of which is a libel as it has no noticeably unpleasant smell but which has elegant deeply cut leaves and drooping green cups edged with red— *H. viridis* is another green flowered species and the rather tender *H. lividus* with flowers of dove-grey flushed with mauve and pink and with a purple flush over the leaves—and the 'Lenten roses'— the so-called *H. orientalis* hybrids—with their nodding bowls of green-shaded-white, apple-blossom and green, plum, wine, and dusky purple, often spotted and peppered with red—all these are excellent ground cover and are useful for their winter and early spring flowers. Once a patch is established few weeds will grow beneath the spread of their handsome evergreen leaves. *Vinca minor*, the periwinkle, in its several varieties is another good evergreen with attractive flowers that makes a dense weed-smothering carpet. To help it to make a compact mass and to flower freely it should be sheared over each year after flowering.

Some people dislike the spotted leaves of *Pulmonaria officinalis*— soldiers and sailors—and of the earlier *P. saccharata* but we think them handsome and approve the Disney-like character they give to the garden throughout the summer. The charm of their croziers of pink and blue flowers is undoubted. *P. rubra* the salmon-red lungwort is the first to flower but, like the glorious *P. angustifolia* 'Mawson's Blue' or 'Munstead', its leaves disappear during the winter months and so its site should be carefully marked. During summer its efficacy as weed smother is undoubted. All these lungworts do well in sun or shade. Not so the omphalodes with their forget-me-not-like blossoms of brilliant blue. Both *Omphalodes verna* and *O. cappodocica* like at least partial shade. In our garden *O. verna* is the first to open and the most rapid of increase although there is no doubt that *O. cappodocica* has the finer flowers.

Another spring flower which is an excellent carpeter for the shrub garden is *Brunnera macrophylla* which gives ample coverage with its leaves and has vivid sky-blue, tiny forget-me-not-like flowers.

Nor should the forget-me-not itself be forgotten. It is one of the prettiest of vernal flowers, although—dying after flowering—it does not give the permanent ground cover of omphalodes and anchusa. If the dying forget-me-not plants are allowed to wither in the ground one need only shake them out as one gathers them for the bonfire or compost-heap, in order to assure an ample crop of seedlings to flower the following year.

With flowers of the forget-me-not kin, nothing looks more charming in a damp spot than the butter-yellow globes of *Trollius europaeus*. The sturdier, golden globe flowers—'Orange Queen' and the like—bloom later, before *Brunnera macrophylla* is over and in time to join the bluebells, either the native *nutans* or *hispanica* which we used to call *Scilla* but which must now be known as *Endymion*.

Later than the anchusa, flowers another borage—*Borago laxiflora* with hairy, rosetted foliage, spreading stems, and graceful pendant turquoise flowers like Chinamen's hats.

Many good flowers are to be found among the borages. The tribe of mertensia—*Mertensia virginica*, the lovely blue cowslip of America; the violet *M. moltkioides*, and the deep blue *M. echioides* and *M. rivularis* var. *japonica* (which last three flower in summer rather than spring)—belong to the borages.

Effortless spreaders, the polemoniums, *Polemonium coeruleum*—Jacob's ladder—and others do well in sun or shade—moist soil or dry. The foot-high, pink flowered *P. carneum* blooms in early summer. 'Blue Pearl' carries its dangling deep blue bells on ten-inch stalks from May to July. The buff-yellow *P. flavum* is rather taller and flowers from July to August while *P. richardsonii* is the most useful and dainty of all, with pretty pinnate foliage and long-stemmed clusters of bright blue, yellow anthered flowers all summer long, from May until September.

To line a path, or to mark a corner in formal paving, the large leathery leaves of the bergenias are excellent. These may in some catalogues still be listed as megasea, but bergenia is the prettier name as well as being the latest edict of the botanists; so by bergenia they shall be known. The old *Bergenia cordifolia* is probably one of the most popular. It often flowers in January, and its rosy spikes of waxy bells are delightful for mixing with the lavender *Iris unguicularis (stylosa)*. The blooms are frost-tender so, to ensure a supply for indoors we now use Polythene cloches to cover a clump or two when frost threatens.

The evening primrose *Oenothera biennis* and the even better *O. lamarckiana* are self-setters which are valuable in the summer garden. Their blooms always remind me of floppy sun-hats and their luminous yellow is something I would not be without. Earlier, in May, the columbines (aquilegias) bloom and their foliage is not the least of their attractions. Their fresh green leaves, something like those of a maidenhair fern, are very decorative and like the fern they help to keep down the weeds. One may start with the long-spurred species and hybrids but as often as not the bees will bring in other pollen and in the end the single or sometimes double 'Granny's Bonnets' will prevail. However, providing one roots out the duller purples and mulberries these will give quite a pleasant effect among shrubs. Of the choicer kinds, the pretty blue hybrid, 'Hensol Harebell' and *Aquilegia canadensis* are best.

The primula family is among the most useful for naturalizing in shrub-belts and of these the yellow wilding and the lilac *Primula altaica* (*P. acaulis rubra*) are among the most useful with us as they flower from November to May in a sheltered corner, asking only a leafy soil and part-shade.

P. denticulata which one so often sees misused in suburban bedding schemes is attractive when planted in drifts and allowed to grow into clumps as the foreground of shrubs. Its large rosettes of leaves help to smother weeds and it is easily increased by division of the crowns in autumn.

P. rosea is charming in a dampish part of the garden. It does not need actual streamside or bog conditions. With us it is quite happy in moist soil at the side of stepping-stones which lead through a shrub-belt between two small lawns. In a similar position we grow the slender *Iris chrysographes* with the 'writing of gold' upon its velvety, purple-black blooms. With its plum-red variety, *I. c.* 'Rubellum', this iris is among the most useful for informal grouping.

To return to the primulas. *Primula japonica, P. pulverulenta, P. bulleyana, P. beesiana, P. cockburniana,* and their other candelabra affinities will do as well in rich, vegetable soil in semi-shade as by the waterside. They are easily raised from seed and will yield interesting variations. From a packet of *P. japonica* seed obtained through the Royal Horticultural Society's seed distribution in 1959 we have plants with flower-heads in brick-red, crimson, and a brilliant and not unpleasing magenta. Of course, where these primulas are grown in colonies, hybridization will creep in, but this only gives a more varied and pleasing colour scheme with all shades and degrees of tiering from white and pink to rose, brick, and crimson with the orange, yellow, flame, and apricot shades included.

Other lovers of dampish soil are the Siberian irises—*Iris sibirica* in variations of blue, purple, and white. Here, I think, the pale blue and the white varieties are the most pleasing. *I.* × *monspur* 'Cambridge Blue' is a distinctive taller growing iris which usually flowers at midsummer. For drier places and at the edge of paths, the six-inch, dwarf bearded irises are appealing in their varieties of white, amber, yellow, and purple.

To some people a geranium is a pelargonium—of harsh colours and coarse growth as seen in public parks and town window-boxes, or even its muted and undeniably attractive ivy-leafed variant. But in the shrub garden we are concerned only with the true geraniums —the species, dense in growth and soft but brilliant in colour, many of which are easy to grow. They spread, and moreover sometimes seed themselves, thus making valuable ground cover as well as providing generous colour splashes in the summer and late summer garden.

Even the familiar *Geranium ibericum* with its large slaty-blue flowers and big leaves may be used to fill in ground between shrubs. It is tough, hardy, and a great spreader. Softer and more appealing with its smaller, silver-pink salvers and equally dense evergreen foliage is *G. endressi* which by hybridizing with other species often gives rise to pleasing variants. The magenta tones of

G. sanguineum, the native 'bloody cranesbill', go well with *G. endressi* and its kin, while another native *G. pratense* is, in its best form, one of the finest herbaceous plants for shrub-garden use. Tall, graceful, and of a soft, deep blue, *G. pratense* occurs in colonies as a wilding in North Wales and along the Border counties. Its favourite station seems to be at the roadsides. Seed taken from a good form of the wild plant will often yield a satisfactory stock for the garden.

G. wallichianum 'Buxton's Blue' is a gem with flowers of a pure nemophila-blue. Eminently suitable for growing among shrubs, being a shade-lover, this geranium is a trailer of which a single plant covers several square feet.

Foxgloves the shrub garden must have, though the good whites and the grape-spotted gloves of the hybrids are more suited to the small garden than the common purple of the wild type. Whether or not I like those hybrids which grow their bells all round the stem I am not sure. I rather think I prefer the form of the earlier hybrids with their bells facing the sun as nature intended.

Campanulas of all kinds associate well with shrubs. The spreading mats of such rockery kinds as *Campanula portenschlagiana (muralis)*, *C. garganica*, *C. turbinata*, and *C. carpatica* form dense ground cover. I usually place a big stone or a rock for them to trail over and they look natural and effective with their starry or bell-like flowers of purple or blue as does the common harebell—the Scottish 'blue-bell', which is surely one of the most charming of all our native wild flowers.

Taller growing campanulas such as *C. persicifolia*, in its white and blue varieties and *C. lactiflora* are pleasing grouped among shrubs and their dense foliage is quite effective as ground cover. In our garden a mixed patch of *C. persicifolia* grown from seed is so good at its job of keeping down undesirables that I can truthfully say we have not had to weed the ground it occupies for the last three years.

Weeds grow in bare, cultivated soil. I mentally groan when tidy-minded gardeners declare that they are going to do away with ground-covering plants so that it will be easier to hoe. Not only is hoeing death to any self-sown seedlings of desirable garden inmates but the crumbly tilth it induces invites every stray weed such as groundsel, plantain, dandelion, and nettle. Moreover, hoeing endangers the roots system of the shrubs and trees, particularly of such surface rooters as rhododendrons, magnolias, azaleas, and camellias. But if the hoe is a menace in the shrub garden how much more so is the fork. I have known gardens ruined in a few years by the fetish 'forking over' that assumes such sacred importance in the eyes of jobbing gardeners and many of their employers. The growth of trees and shrubs is hindered by recurrent root damage. The soil structure is ruined—humus vanishes, and forked-over soils become unyielding, dust-dry, and without heart. Bulbs and cherished plants either die from drought or are murdered by the fork. Then, to complete the cycle of disaster, the despairing garden owner listens to the jobbing gardener's advice to lime the garden 'to sweeten the soil'! So are good gardens ruined and men and women of good faith driven to tear their hair. If I had my way I would banish fork, hoe, and lime from every shrub garden in the land.

Many plants and shrubs will, you will find, do much better for cooling comfort of a slab of stone on the surface above their roots. Daphnes, clematis, heaths, azaleas, and dwarf rhododendrons all like to send their roots under the stone to seek the moisture it retains. It serves also to anchor the roots and protect the plant from wind-rock. In our windswept garden we use boulders to anchor the roots of broom, ceanothus, and *Cupressus macrocarpa*. Any plant which shows signs of being loosened by the wind at once has a heavy stone placed to windward of its stem. Care must be taken, however, not to use limestone rock in conjunction with lime-hating plants.

Hepaticas and double primroses are treasures which associate well with flowering shrubs but which sometimes prove difficult to establish. We find that both do well if planted between flat slabs of stone in semi-shade. We planted ramondas in the same spot and they seem happy there and have gone on to form large clumps. The double primroses have to be divided every two or three years and this necessitates raising the stones, so we take the opportunity to replace the soil with leaf-mould, loam, and cow-manure. The hepaticas, of course, must remain undisturbed. They appreciate sharper drainage than do the primulas and when planting them it is as well to incorporate grit and leaf-mould with the soil. Unlike the primroses they dislike manure.

At first thought, stone may seem out of place in a shrub garden but in reality it blends well. We use rocks to give height and a raised effect to what might otherwise be rather flat beds of dwarf rhododendrons, azaleas, and *Linum narbonense* and the plants do well because of the shade and moisture which the rocks afford their roots. Strategically placed rocks heighten the effect of brooms such as *Cytisus×kewensis* and also the genista *lydia*, and *Cytisus praecox*. Lithospermum needs stone over which it may tumble, and its brilliant blue shows up best against certain honey coloured slabs that we find on the sea-shore.

If you aspire to grow the petiolaris primulas—*Primula edgeworthii* and *P. bhutanica*—between the crevices of a north-facing, dry wall or between rock edgings is the place for them. They need to be planted on their sides so that the winter moisture will run from their rosettes and not settle in the crowns to cause rot. However, I have seen *P. edgeworthii* growing happily between the roots of an old tree; and in the Savill Gardens in Windsor Great Park this connoisseur's pet thrives between logs edging a woodsy, leaf-mould bed surrounding a tree, while some of their fellows do well enough on the flat surface of the bed. I suspect the reason for this is that overhanging tree-branches keep off any excess of winter moisture.

When a shrub garden is first planted there must inevitably be gaps between the shrubs, spaces which they will fill when they attain their full growth. In the meantime the ground must be kept mulched and weeded. We find such operations much simplified if large flat stones are placed to serve as stepping-stones in the bed.

Our garden is mainly flat, and rather than interfere with the soil-levels we decided to keep it that way. The flatness is relieved in one part by a stepping-stone path between slightly raised beds containing half-buried rocks against which Kurume azaleas, heaths, the rhododendron 'Blue Tit', *Geranium endressi*, and *Pulmonaria angustifolia* nestle. These plants all have the appearance of extreme

9. *Embothrium lanceolatum*, slender and upright like a flame, with tomato-scarlet flowers in June

10. *Eucalyptus niphophila* (Snow Gum) grown as a pruned shrub will fit in well with the small shrub garden scheme

11. *Euonymus latifolius,* one of the finest of the spindle-berries

12a. *Escallonia* 'Donard Seedling' is pretty in bud with flesh-pink flowers that open white

12b. *Fabiana imbricata* 'Prostrata' is an appealing, semi-hardy prostrate shrub for mild districts. It will grow well on a sunny bank in poor soil

13. *Hamamelis mollis* 'Pallida' a distinctive Witch Hazel with telling pale-yellow flowers

14. *Hebe* (Veronica) 'Midsummer Beauty', a summer shrub for all but the most exposed gardens

15. *Hibiscus sino-syraciacus* is a late-summer subject for full sun

16. *Hipphophae rhamnoides*, the Sea Buckthorn, is a grey-foliaged, deciduous shrub that will grow in poor soils and exposed situations near the sea. The female plants bear colourful orange berries in autumn and winter, but to obtain a good display both sexes must be grown

good health, due I am sure to the extra root-moisture and the protection which the rocks give.

Some people feel they must have a splash of bedding colour even in a shrub garden and the way in which this can be achieved without affecting anybody's susceptibilities is to fill stone troughs or sinks, ornamental metal tanks or wooden troughs, with wall-flowers, petunias, and antirrhinums in season, confining them to the terrace or sitting-out place, or to the immediate surrounds of the house.

I have developed this theme in my book *Window Box and Container Gardening*, suggesting the decoration of patios, balconies and terraces with flower-filled containers that leave the main rhythm of the shrub garden undisturbed.

16

Bulbs to Naturalize

Everyone loves bulbous plants and luckily they look as well and as much at home in the shrub garden as in any other. Some, such as the snowdrop and certain of the daffodils, seem even more so.

It is difficult to decide when the bulb year starts. I like to think of it as beginning in August when the bulb catalogues arrive and when one plants autumn crocuses and colchicums and indeed any other bulbs that come to hand, because the sooner they are all in the ground the better.

The true autumn crocuses are slender little plants which need a sheltered spot among the shrubs where the first autumn storm will not flatten them. The two easiest and cheapest species will satisfy the average gardener's desire for a foretaste of spring in September. The rosy-mauve *Crocus zonatus* is the first to flower, followed by the deep blue, orange stigmaed *C. speciosus*. Both of these will seed and naturalize freely where the absence of hoeing permits. They may be planted in rough grass, in the soil of a shrub belt, or in cracks among paving. An initial purchase of two or three dozen of each will yield increasing drifts of colour over the years.

The colchicums, too, are sometimes known as autumn crocuses, although the misleading 'meadow saffron' is perhaps the more commonly used term. They differ from the crocuses entirely in botanical detail, belonging in fact to the lily family whereas the crocus belongs to that of the iris. Superficially, however, in garden appearance they show cousinhood. Colchicum bulbs are large and each throws up a profusion of long-necked chalices in mauve, purple, or white. The blooms of some—notably *Colchicum agrippinum*—are chequered like those of the fritillary and have a most unusual and attractive appearance.

Unfortunately colchicum leaves are coarse and appear in spring. Colchicums, therefore, are best planted in rough grass or among ferns where the huge, strap-like leaves will not be too noticeable. This advice is only for the super-tidy-minded gardener. For my part I like the leaves; they are evidence that the bulbs are thriving. They assist them to store food to aid the summer's flower production and surely no gardener worthy of the name can call any foliage 'untidy'. However, I have heard it said—and by people who should know better—that they will not tolerate even daffodils in their gardens because their leaves are so *untidy*! When I hear sentiments like this I despair. Are we becoming so pernickety as to let neatness rather than beauty become the criterion by which we judge a garden?

The schizostylises—red *Schizostylis coccinea*; silver-pink 'Viscountess Byng', and the brighter 'Mrs. Hegarty'—like miniature gladioli, are easy autumn-flowering bulbs for sunny, well-drained parts of the garden. In cold districts they may need to be planted under a south wall but here in the West they are hardy. Nothing in the autumn garden gives me more pleasure than a clump of the warm pink 'Mrs. Hegarty' growing behind a mat of brilliant blue *Ceratostigma wilmottianum* on a low bank.

Snowdrops may be had in October if you plant *Galanthus olgae* in a sunny, stony place, but this species and the spring-flowering large-flowered *G. nivalis* 'S. Arnott' and the January '*Atkinsii*' are treasures for special places. For naturalizing in generous drifts, the ordinary *G. nivalis* and *G. elwesii* are best and certainly the least expensive. Often people find snowdrops difficult to establish. We did in our present garden until we planted freshly lifted bulbs as they went out of flower. Specialist snowdrop firms will supply them in this state as it is the most likely to ensure success.

Snowflakes—*Leucojum vernum* and its varieties—are, like the rarer snowdrops, too expensive and choice to plant other than in small groups in selected spots where they are frequently seen and where watchful care may be exercised over them.

Of the many early-flowering crocus species and varieties, the best, we find, for ordinary garden purposes and for naturalizing among shrubs or in grass are the amethyst *Crocus tomasinianus* with its small starry cups with their vivid orange stigmas, its varieties 'Barr's Purple', 'Whitewell Purple', and 'Taplow Ruby'; mixed batches of *C. chrysanthus* which give an amazing colour range of gold, brown, lemon, cream, marigold, blue, and purple feathered varieties, and the lavender *C. vernus* which will hybridize freely with *C. tomasinianus* and yield some interesting variants.

The larger Dutch crocuses—the 'fat boys', as Reginald Farrer called them—are good to follow on, and are best planted in groups and drifts of separate colours.

Mice are often troublesome in stealing crocus corms but we have found that they never touch those planted in grass. A word of warning is necessary here, because grass in which bulbs are planted must not be cut until the foliage has died down in June. Otherwise the bulbs, deprived of their source of food-supply from their leaves, will starve and eventually die.

Daffodils of the mammoth class look out of proportion in a small shrub garden. They need to be planted in swathes across broad grassland or under the trees of an old orchard if they are not to appear out of scale. Small species such as the early *Narcissus cyclamineus* with its shy-eared flowers will do well in moist yet well-drained places. A streamside or a partly shaded spot in damp, sandy soil encourages them to naturalize. More open spots will suit the dwarf, hoop-petticoat *N. bulbocodium*.

One of the best, strongest growing, and most freely increasing small daffodils is *N. obvallaris*—the Tenby daffodil—with shapely golden trumpets on ten-inch stems. The native Lent lily—*N. pseudo-narcissus*—has enchanting small flowers with deep yellow trumpets and paler, twisted perianths. It takes longer to establish and to become free-flowering than does the Tenby daffodil which usually blooms prolifically in its first spring.

For naturalizing in orchards or wide stretches of grass where larger daffodils would be in keeping, such varieties as the large-cupped 'Carlton', 'John Evelyn' with its frilly cup of pale apricot, the early trumpets 'Magnificence' and 'Flower Carpet', and the much later *N. recurvus*—the 'Pheasant's Eye' *N. poeticus*—are all strong growers which will do well and increase easily.

Some people like to naturalize Darwin tulips in grass. To my eye they never look right there. Tulips for the shrub garden are best restricted to such species as *Tulip eichleri* and *T. praestans* 'Fusilier' in scarlet; the candy striped *T. clusiana*; the smaller of the *kaufmanniana* hybrids; *T. sylvestris*, our own quaint wild tulip with its early yellow flowers, and the brilliant but expensive *T. sprengeri* which is latest to flower. All these are not, however, bulbs to grow in grass. They should be planted from six to eight inches deep in sunny, well-drained places where they can remain undisturbed. They are among the few plants which seem to need added lime if they are to be permanent and I think this may best be supplied in the form of ground limestone. Needless to say, tulip species so treated must be kept away from any lime-hating plants.

At the same time as the tulips, the garden bluebells flower. The white, pink, and blue *hispanica* forms are the most suitable for shrub-garden planting where they will increase freely in sun or shade.

While dealing with scillas we must not forget the earlier *Scilla bifolia* nor *Scilla siberica* and those useful allies the chionodoxas with which *bifolia* occasionally hybridizes. Muscari, too, grape hyacinths, in blue or white, are charming and rapid colonizers, but the larger hyacinths have, in my opinion, no possible place in the shrub garden, being much too stocky and formal in appearance. Grow them, by all means, in bowls for the house and enjoy their scent, but spare the garden the embarrassment of their over-opulent presence.

The fritillarias with drooping, slender-stemmed bells of chequered purple or white look as if they might have been carried by one of Titania's fairies, yet they are robust enough to colonize in grass or between shrubs. *Fritillaria meleagris* is the easiest to grow and a purchase of mixed bulbs will yield every variation.

Flowering in early summer, *Camassia cusickii* carries four-foot spikes of starry, grey-blue flowers above broad foliage. With the deep mauve-blue *C. leichthenii atroviolacea* and the smaller rich blue *C. esculenta* it offers a succession to the Spanish bluebells.

Later still *Galtonia candicans* carries stems of heavy snow-white bells which will justify the name 'Summer Hyacinth' and make a majestic group among shrubs.

Alliums, belonging to the onion family, have a reputation for unpleasant smells. However, most ornamental garlics found in gardens give off no odour unless the stems are broken or bruised. Some may even be used for cutting for the house without offence. Among the cheapest and easiest are the foot-high June-flowering *Allium moly* with umbels of golden flowers; *A. ostrowskianum* which is only six inches high but with its pretty deep rose flower-heads makes an attractive drift for the front of shrubs in June, and *A. sphaerocephalum* which flowers from June to July with round, dense heads of lilac-purple. Also in July, flowers the two-foot *A. azureum* with deep blue flower-umbels. More expensive but worth the price to form a showy group among rhododendrons or other shrubs, the evergreen *A. rosenbachianum* carries bright purple-rose, globe-shaped heads on stout, four-foot stems in May.

The giant gladiolus has no place in the shrub garden. Permissible for groups in the more formal border are the early summer-flowering *Gladiolus colvillei* hybrids of which 'The Bride' and 'Peach Blossom' are lovely. They are not strong enough growers to naturalize and need a sheltered, well-drained spot if they are to be truly perennial.

Of the more uncommon bulbs, certain of the dog's tooth violets —the erythroniums—are among the most charming and easy to naturalize. Better than the European *Erythronium dens-canis* varieties, which we find rather dumpy and slow to open in the wan March sunshine, are the Californian species *E. californicum* 'Giganteum' and the true *E. revolutum* which is an airy flowered rose-pink, sometimes listed as *E. r.* 'Johnsonii'. These all flower on six- to ten-inch stems and their turkscap flowers have a lily-like grace. They are admittedly somewhat expensive to buy from the bulb-dealers in autumn, but at least one enterprising firm has begun to import the bulbs from America in early summer as was frequently done in pre-war days. Purchased in this way before they have dried off, they are cheaper and will establish more readily. Indeed, all the species mentioned will increase freely in moist peaty soil in a partially shaded spot. Seed sown as soon as ripe in a moist, semi-shaded part of the garden will germinate the following April as freely as mustard and cress. Unfortunately plants raised in this way take five years to flower.

17

Garden Treasures

Chief among garden joys for the enthusiast are the small treasures which need a little coddling, or at any rate need to be planted in exactly suitable conditions of soil—acid or neutral, damp or dry—in sun or in shade—and which must at all costs be spared the careless hoe or fork. Like sensitive children they need 'individual attention'.

Of these my special spring favourites are the anemones—most of which, apart from the flamboyant coronarias, are suitable for growing among shrubs. *Anemone blanda* from Greece with its large, daisy-petalled flowers in various blues from near-indigo to prussian and gentle sky, rose, paler pink, and white, is the earliest to flower, often beginning its season in a sunny spot in February. Later *A. apennina* opens its smaller yet similar flowers in bright, rich blue or white and, liking shade, is good to plant with the enchanting dog's tooth violets mentioned in the foregoing chapter.

Where happy, *A. blanda* and *A. apennina* will colonize as freely as our native wood anemone *A. nemorosa* which incidentally looks charming among shrubs and which may be obtained in several blue varieties notably the pale lavender *A. n.* 'Robinsoniana', powder-blue *A. n.* 'Allenii', and the richer 'Royal Blue' in addition to the starry white of the woodlands.

One of the most appealing of all anemones is *A. hepatica*, the liverwort, with its leathery, three-lobed or rounded leaves and meek blooms of clear blue, rose, or white with their tufts of snowy stamens. Whether one cares for the double forms of this species or not is a matter of taste. Sometimes I think that the pose of despising all double flowers is a form of snobbery. It is hard to see why anyone should object to the double pink or blue hepaticas, whose rosetted flowers have the simplicity and old-fashioned charm of the double primrose which even the purists find acceptable. For my part I shall continue to grow every double hepatica that I have the good fortune to discover.

Double or single, the hepaticas enjoy cool, woodland conditions. They need some shade and thrive best in well-drained, gritty yet moisture-holding soils. A generous quantity of beech-mould and grit mixed well into the proposed planting site is the best recipe for success.

Apart from *A. hepatica* in its various forms there is also *A. h. angulosa*, now, by some obscure ruling of the botanists, to be known as *A. transsilvanica*. This species is found wild only in Hungary. It is a bigger flowered plant, but it lacks the white stamens of the common hepatica which contrast so well with the pinks and blues, and it is not so easy to cultivate. In my experience it does not flower so freely; whereas *A. hepatica* will quickly form cushions of bloom. *A. transsilvanica* seems to yield no more than three or four sulky flowers, whose size does not compensate for the quantity and undoubted charm of those of its more free-and-easy relative. *A. transsilvanica* has, however, given us a valuable hybrid with the common hepatica. This is *A.* × *intermedia* 'Ballard's Variety', which carries wide, clear blue blooms on five-inch stalks and has lost none of the quality of the species.

The pasque flower is another of the anemone clan which makes a suitable and decorative addition to the shrub garden. But while the hepaticas are happy in semi-shade, the pulsatilla (formerly known as *A. pulsatilla* and now as *Pulsatilla vulgaris*) needs a more open, well-drained site; a low bank in front of shrubs is ideal, or the foreground of a slightly raised bed. Although found wild on our chalk downs, in cultivation the pasque flower does equally well in acid soil.

While our native pulsatilla has drooping bells of purple, varieties are obtainable in many different shades, some with much larger flowers. All have the same golden anthers and silky furred buds and stems. Among some of the best are the rich, glowing pink 'Mrs. Van der Elst'; the pale blue 'John Innes Variety'; *P. alba*, which is snowy white in its good form; *P. farreri*, a violet; *P. caucasica*, a pale yellow of fairly recent introduction; and 'Budapest', which is perhaps the most useful of all, flowering as it does in February or early March. In its best forms 'Budapest' is a true, clear blue with starry, bell-shaped flowers which open flat in the sunshine to reveal the fine stamens.

No less lovely is *Anemone alpina* 'Sulphurea'—now, I believe, to be known as *Pulsatilla alpina* 'Sulphurea'—with its soft yellow bells swaddled in an outer covering of tawny fur. This, like *Pulsatilla vulgaris* and the hepaticas, thrives with us in cool, well-drained soil with a high humus content.

Another family of shy and endearing wildings are the hardy cyclamen with their small shuttlecock-heads and the air of startled deer.

Even those of us who have not come upon these cyclamen in the beauty of their natural environment, under the trees on some Greek islet, or caught their perfume wafted across the waters of a Swiss lake, still sigh with pleasure when we come upon a patch nestling between the tree-roots in an English garden.

Often in old gardens one sees *Cyclamen neapolitanum* with corms as large as a breakfast plate, bearing forty or fifty elegant flowers above a nest of marbled, ivy-shaped leaves. This cyclamen is in appearance an exact miniature of the greenhouse giants which grace our houses at Christmas. It flowers in late August, September, and on through October. The type species bears blooms of pale rosy-pink, their reflexed petals turned back to show a ring of crimson at the centre of the flower. Still more appealing is the rarer white variety *C. n. album*, which may have the same crimson marking at the heart or be unsullied in the chasteness of its white.

Both these cyclamen are good 'doers', in spite of anything one may have heard to the contrary. Once established in a place they like they will thrive and naturalize themselves freely by self-sown seedlings. The only difficulty lies in their establishment. After years of trying to obtain a cyclamen patch by buying dormant corms in the late autumn we came to the conclusion that it is more satisfactory, although initially more expensive, to buy the flowering plants in minute pots in September and to plant them directly into the ground. Bought in this manner the type will cost perhaps twenty-five pence a corm, while the white variety may be double that—but what is fifty pence reckoned against a lifetime of yearly beauty?

Cyclamen may also be grown with reasonable success from seed sown *in situ*. Choose a site in semi-shade; the base of an oak or beech tree is ideal. Sow the seed thinly and cover with half an inch of sifted soil and leaf-mould. Here, if the hoe is banned, the seeds will germinate and will in time give you your desired carpet of hardy cyclamen.

Earlier than *C. neapolitanum* to flower is *C. europaeum*, the plant of Swiss woods and lakesides. This has a smaller bloom than *C. neapolitanum* and is perhaps less elegantly shaped, but there is infinite appeal in the tiny rose-crimson blooms, and a world of enchantment in the haunting scent. It is, however, more susceptible to frost and may do better in stony soil in full sun than in the shady spots beloved by *C. neapolitanum*.

Cyclamen may be had in flower nearly all the year round. Even at Christmas I have the outdoor flowers of *C. orbiculatum* 'Atkinsii', with sombre, rounded leaves and bluntly shaped flowers in rose and white. *C. o. coum* flowers also in December and January; it has similar leaves with white or rose-crimson shuttlecocks to cheer us at a time of year when we need it most.

All of these cyclamen seem to do best in a slightly shady position in good leafy soil, and they appreciate an annual mulching with leaf mould. Although they are reputed to like lime I have never given any to my plants, and they do not seem to notice its absence. *C. libanoticum*, however, a February flowerer, is not so easy to please. In sheltered parts of the country it will flower out of doors, but it is not reliable hardy and is really a plant for the Alpine house, or at least a subject for cloche protection during winter frosts. Fuchsine-pink in flower colour, this cyclamen is most attractive, with slender, elongated petals zoned with crimson. It likes chalk, and in this climate needs a hot, sunny position.

Wholly satisfactory outdoors is a later spring-flowering cyclamen —*C. repandum*, with deep carmine blossoms. *Vernum (orbiculatum)* is also carmine, with deeper spot: either is delightful when it joins the throng of spring with flowers which are fairly large, slender, and deep-hued. Like most of its kin, *C. repandum* will do well at the base of a tree.

One point applies to all the hardy cyclamen. They should not be too deeply planted but tipped out of their pots into the prepared holes with their bases just level with the surrounding soil. A little leaf-mould may then be scattered over the corms. Too-deep planting is a common cause of failure.

Gentians are among the treasures many people would like to grow—the spring-flowering *Gentiana acaulis* and *G. verna* in sunny spots between shrubs, and the autumn-flowering Asiatics in peaty, lime-free beds in partial shade.

To many people, a gentian means the gentianella, the Swiss *G. acaulis* with its large trumpets of deep violet-blue. Yet this is just the gentian which is the most temperamental of all. With some people it does so well as to be almost an embarrassment, while others can grow it easily enough but with them it will not flower. Many theories have been put forward in attempts to solve the mystery. Some say that various garden forms are more free-flowering than others. Others say that to cultivate *G. acaulis* successfully one must import quantities of the soil from a garden where it thrives. Yet others insist on a regular trampling in stiff loam. My own belief is that it needs a well-drained, shaly soil and full sun. I believe, too, that over-frequent division is bad. *G. acaulis* should be allowed to spread rapidly as in nature. And, if it will on no account do for you, try the other spring gentian, the lower growing *G. verna* with its intensely blue trumpets. *G. verna* is occasionally found wild in this country. It used to be found in much greater numbers before so-called 'flower-lovers' collected it to perish in the white crystalline graveyards that our Victorian grandfathers knew as 'rockeries'.

G. verna needs careful soil preparation. It thrives in a sandy loam with plenty of leaf-mould incorporated. Even so it is not reliably permanent and should be raised regularly from seed.

In growing gentians from seed we strike another peculiarity. Like many alpines they should be sown in autumn in pans which are allowed to spend the winter beneath a north-facing hedge or wall. The seeds need exposure to frost and snow. They have to undergo the freezing and thawing they would encounter in their natural habitat if they are to germinate.

So far we have been thinking of gentians in terms of difficulty and uncertainty, but there are other—some equally beautiful—members of the genus which may be ranked among the horticultural 'easies'.

Such is the magnificent autumn-flowering G. *sino-ornata* with its immense trumpets of dark, brilliant blue which form sheets and drifts of colour from September until December. G. *sino-ornata* needs a lime-free soil. It appreciates peat or leaf-mould and is best planted from thonged roots in the spring. Once established it is readily increased by detaching rooted shoots in May. These, dibbled into suitable soil, will have grown into flowering plants by September.

If your soil is chalky or limed, the glories of G. *sino-ornata* are not for you. There are alternatives, slightly less glamorous but, none the less, serviceable and easy. One of the best of these is the August-flowering G. *septemfida* with its profusion of smaller but, nevertheless, appealing bright blue trumpets which are carried in clusters that are ideal for cutting.

Other good gentians are the hybrids; G. ×*macaulayi* 'Well's Variety' with its large blue trumpets brilliantly striped in green and purple—the true peacock of the family, this one; 'Kidbrooke Seedling', an improved G. *sino-ornata* and propagated in the same manner (I always give this gentian the same treatment as G. *sino-ornata* in a bed of leaf-mould and peat but I have been told that it does equally well in a limy soil), and G. *farreri*, another Asiatic with Cambridge-blue, white throated trumpets borne from August to September, said by some to tolerate lime.

To the gardener whose soil is chalky it must be irritating to read so often of treasures which need lime-free soil. However, there are many glorious garden plants which do perfectly well on lime or chalk, provided suitable growing conditions are supplied.

Apart from the lilacs, mock oranges, flowering cherries, and crabs which thrive when lime is present there are many of the smaller garden gems—the little treasures that perhaps give the gardener the greatest pleasure of all—which are perfectly happy in an alkaline medium. One of these is the lady's slipper orchid, which is still a native of at least one place in the north of England, although plants nowadays are usually imported from the Continent where their habitat has not been so reduced by the predatory activities of self-styled 'flower-lovers'.

Cypripedium calceolus is a charming plant with baggy pouched 'slippers' in deep yellow, and chocolate-maroon petals and sepals, carried on twelve-inch stems above lily-of-the-valley-like foliage in June. This is a plant which does best where lime is present and I have known many attempts to grow it in favoured, acid-soiled rhododendron gardens which have ended in failure. Give the lady's slipper leaf-mould and limestone grit in a partly shaded spot and it will be happy. Do not, however, go to extremes over the shade. Semi-shade is necessary but the plant definitely needs some sunlight. The dappled shade of overhanging shrubs or trees is ideal.

Rhodothamnus chamaecistus is a dwarf shrub which many connoisseurs would be content to grow well. It comes from the limestone mountains of the Austrian Alps, but it will grow happily in either acid or alkaline conditions provided that one meets its basic needs of semi-shade and incorporates a generous amount of moisture-holding peat and leaf-mould in the soil. In my own mind I am not sure to what extent it needs shade. Plants in dense shade flower less freely than those in more open conditions, and I rather feel that shade from the midday sun which might fade the clear rose of its wide open bells is all that is necessary provided the plant is well supplied with the essential moisture at its roots. Peaty soil with surface slabs of limestone makes this practicable.

Many primulas, especially the candelabra types, are only truly at home in peaty, acid soils; yet there are other equally lovely and desirable members of the genus which thrive among the limestone rocks of retaining walls or edging. Chief of these, of auricula type, is 'Linda Pope', with handsome leaves and cool lilac flowers, while 'Mrs. G.F. Wilson' and 'Faldonside' are also good.

Meconopsis (apart from the single orange and yellow Welsh poppies—*Meconopsis cambrica*—which we think pretty, although undoubtedly a weed, and leave to seed wherever they will in the garden) need an acid soil if their colours are to be pure. The lovely 'blue poppy', *M. betonicifolia*, is not perennial if allowed to flower in its second year from seed. Bought yearling plants should have their flowering stems nipped out from the base so that they will then make secondary basal rosettes and become strong clumps to flower for their second and succeeding seasons. *M. grandis* is larger and even more beautiful than *M. betonicifolia*—kingfisher-blue in its best forms—and it is a true perennial. The basic need of all meconopsis is a cool humus-containing soil and part-shade.

Fabiana imbricata 'Prostrata' is an appealing semi-hardy prostrate shrub for mild districts: it grows well on a sunny bank in poor soil. There is a blue-violet form *violacea* which is even more pleasing than the type.

Lilies are treasures *par excellence* for the small shrub garden. Many are easy and are ideal for planting among dwarf evergreen azaleas and other low-growing shrubs where the shrub growth will shade the lower parts of their stems leaving the buds and upper stems open to the sun. Specially suited to this method of culture are the stem-rooting lilies. The spring and summer mulches which benefit the azaleas help the lily-stems to root as they grow while the azalea-stems and leaves help to protect the lily-shoots from spring frosts.

Lilium croceum, the orange cottage lily; *L. umbellatum* with its upright funnels in varying shades of orange and gold; golden throated *L. regale* with its white trumpets banded on the outside with vinous purple, and the flamboyant, late summer- and autumn-flowering *L. tigrinum* are all suited to grow in this way.

We have talked a lot about plants which dislike alkaline soils. This is true of some of the lilies, but *L. henryi* with its orange-yellow, reflexed flowers and the dainty *L. pomponium* with its sealing-wax red turkscaps will not do well in an acid soil. Lilies which thrive on chalky or limed soils include the well-known Madonna lily, *L. candidum* (which should always be planted in August or September), *L. croceum, L.*×*dalhansonii, L. davidii, L. giganteum, L. hansonii, L. martagon, L.*×*maxwill*, the scarce and expensive *L. monadelphum, L. pardalinum, L. pyrenaicum, L. regale, L.*

$\times$ *testaceum*, and *L. umbellatum*, although few of these object to acidity in the way in which *L. henryi* and *L. pomponium* do and will always be grateful for the addition of leaf-mould or humus to the soil.

All lilies need good drainage and should never be planted in stagnant ground. Heavy soil should be lightened by adding leaf-mould and sand, and it is advisable always to put a handful of sand beneath the base of the bulb when planting. Suitable spring mulches are leaf-mould and well-rotted manure or compost. Bone-meal helps to build up a strong, free-flowering bulb while bracken placed over the site of the bulbs in winter will help to keep off the frost and will provide a valuable food as it rots. Lilies which we grow among shrubs are *L. regale*; the heavily scented, spotted, early yellow turkscap *L. pyrenaicum*; *L. martagon album* with its chaste, reflexed flowers; the September-flowering *L. speciosum* and its glamorous varieties; the brilliant July-flowering *L. willmottiae* (a variety of *L. davidii*) which sometimes carries as many as forty flowers on stems which may reach from four to seven feet in height, and *L. tigrinum*.

For shady places among shrubs the late May-flowering trilliums, the wood lilies of North America—picturesquely known as 'Wake Robin'—are appealing. Both the dull red and white varieties of *Trillium grandiflorum* are good. Another charming plant from the same continent is the Canadian blood-root—*Sanguinaria canadensis*—in its single and double forms. The single form is particularly beautiful with its milk-white anemone-like flower pushing up from a scrolled, bluish grey leaf. Liking the same conditions of cool, woodsy, acid soil among shrubs the Canadian dogwood, *Cornus canadensis*, is a vigorous carpeter with showy, bracted white flowers followed in good years by glowing autumn foliage colour.

Some new strains of lily hybrids from America are less prone to virus diseases than are the species and older hybrids. The Harlequins and Fiesta and Backhouse hybrids look particularly at home among shrubs; the Golden Clarion and Moonlight strains are lovely too, with trumpet-flowers in shades of lemon to gold and lime-yellow respectively. Cheshire Bulb Farms Ltd (see p.197) are now raising the ultra-hardy and virus-resistant Canadian Patterson hybrids in this country.

18

Climbers

Small shrub gardens usually offer attractive and varied sites for the many lovely climbing plants which will grow freely in this country. Not only are the walls of house, garage, and garden shed available for their support but often there are old trees, either evergreen or deciduous, already on the site whose branches will act as host to the less rampant climbers without detriment to themselves. Old apple trees, worthless in fruit, provide spring blossom on their own account and make excellent frameworks through which the large-flowered clematises may ramble. Hedges, too, may be used in this way. Yew, holly, cupressus, or any other evergreen will be enhanced by the planting of the tuberous-rooted flame flower *Tropaeolum speciosum* to scramble against the dark background of their foliage. *T. speciosum* in general does better in the north and west of the country than in the drier and hotter south. To succeed it should be planted in moist, peaty soil on the north side of the evergreen up which it is to climb and, when really happy, it will spread rapidly—running underground and appearing to brighten the sides of paths and other places with its gay scarlet, little nasturtium flowers. When planting climbers to interweave through other plants it is necessary to prepare an area a couple of feet from the proposed host and to enrich the soil before planting the climber and leading it by means of a slender cane to the start of its ascent. *Mutisia oligodon* is a climber of a different type. Instead of having tuberous roots that creep underground like the tropaeolums, the mutisias grow like clematises from fibrous roots and must be planted out from pots. They do, however, throw up suckers which may be carefully detached in April to make new plants. *M. oligodon* is one of the hardiest of a somewhat tender genus. It is a lovely plant with wide rayed, reflexing, large daisy flowers in a clear and shining pink and tiny, dull, holly-like leaves that climbs by means of tendrils and like the flame flower needs moist, peaty soil. It may be planted against a wall or fence, preferably in company with a rose or other climber through which it may scramble, or on the north side of an evergreen shrub. Whichever site is chosen its roots must be kept cool. Provided this need is met (by means of a slab of stone or a protective clump of catmint) it will thrive even against a south-facing wall. Some authorities say that it is impossible to strike the mutisias from cuttings but I have several times been successful with *M. oligodon*, choosing internoded cuttings in April and rooting them under glass—in the east-facing window of an unheated room—in a compost of peat and loam. Each time the cuttings blackened off at the top and appeared to be dead but I kept up the watering and eventually the green young shoots emerged. All the cuttings rooted have made vigorous plants.

Many clematis are more satisfactory when allowed to climb through a host plant than when trained up wire or trellis against a wall. We grow our clematis through climbing roses and find this a satisfactory means both of supporting the clematis and of prolonging the display. 'Ville de Lyon' (crimson), 'Jackmannii' (purple), 'Lasurstern' (deep blue), 'Comtesse de Chambaud' (pink), 'Duchess of Edinburgh' (double white), 'Lady Northcliffe' (lavender-blue), 'Prince Hendrick' (very large blue), 'Nelly Moser' (pale pink with a deeper bar) are all reliable large-flowered hybrids from which a selection may be made. Very attractive and extremely free-flowering are the small-flowered *Clematis viticella* varieties 'Abundance' and *C. v.* 'Kermesina'. Useful species are the spring-flowering *C. montana* and *C. m. rubens* which will curtain a tree with their veils of white or pink starry flowers. *C. chrysocoma* is better still with larger pink flowers from May to August. For a warm wall the Chinese evergreen, *C. armandii* 'Apple Blossom' is lovely in April and worth accommodating on a length of pig-wire, suspended from an upper-story window-frame or from the eaves of the house, so that its handsome foliage may be seen to advantage.

C. macropetala with its shaggy powder-blue double flowers in spring is an attractive scrambler, seen at its best rambling over bushes of lavender or rosemary or climbing over a small evergreen. *C. tangutica obtusiuscula* is a deciduous species, flowering in July and August with pendant lemon-yellow bells. This species is charming when rambling through an evergreen or over a low stone wall. An additional attraction are the skye-terrier-like silky seed-heads that follow the flowers and are useful for interior decoration in autumn.

Clematis prefer to have their roots on the north side of a fence or shrub and to climb over into the sun, but if grown in full sun their roots must be shaded by a dwarf shrub or large stone.

Large trees and even apple trees offer suitable supports for climbing roses of the old-fashioned rambler type and for rose species. Where old apple trees are to be used, however, it is as well first to kill the trees by removing a complete girdle of bark from the trunks. Such roses as the creamy yellow 'Goldfinch', 'Amethyste', the nodding 'Félicité et Perpétue', and 'The Garland' are all suitable. In warm districts the double Banksian rose with its small yellow rosettes is a charming May-flowerer. It is important not to prune back the Banksian roses because they flower on old wood and if they were cut back one would have no flowers. The other roses mentioned should have the old wood cut out from the base occasionally. Other good roses to plant against trees are the creamy-white 'Mme Plantière', pale pink 'New Dawn', the free-flowering, May-October-blooming 'Zéphirine Drouhin', and the lovely, quilted 'Gloire de Dijon' whose buff-apricot flowers have a true tea fragrance.

Startling and baroque, and able to climb up to twenty feet, is the double-flowered, magenta crimson *Rosa russelliana*, while for a really big tree, or to scramble over a hedge, the huge heads of small creamy-white flowers of *R. filipes* 'Kiftsgate' with their orangey-yellow centres of stamens and pervading scent create a striking effect in June. Good, too, for a hedge is 'Mermaid', well known for the beauty of its large, single, pale yellow flowers and amber stamens.

Climbing roses grown up trees will need the support of wire

hoops, fastened round to prevent them being blown loose by the wind.

For walls, climbing roses of the hybrid tea, and China classes are the most suitable as they are less subject to mildew than the rambling type which always seem to suffer from this trouble when grown in a dry position. Suitable varieties are 'Lady Hillingdon' (copper tea), 'Souvenir de Claudius Denoyel' (crimson hybrid tea), 'Climbing Hermosa' (pink China), 'Climbing Cramoisie Supérieure' (crimson China), 'Alister Stella Grey' (yellow noisette), 'Allen Chandler' (single scarlet hybrid tea). The Banksian roses are particularly suitable for warm, sunny walls as are the well-known South of France roses, 'La Follette' (warm pink), the vivid 'Ramona' (huge single crimson-lake with pale reverses to the petals), 'Belle Portugaise' (flesh-pink), and the rich yellow 'Claire Jacquier'.

It should be stressed at this point that roses, and indeed any other plants which are to be grown against walls must be planted in well-prepared and enriched sites. The holes should be at least two feet square and two spades deep. All the original soil should be removed as this is inevitably poor and often limy. In its place, turf loam, peat, and compost would be ideal. It should be remembered that the soil against walls is liable to become very dry, and frequent copious watering is necessary during dry spells.

Honeysuckles are good to cover old dead trees, to climb up sheds or porches, or even to intertwine in rough hedges. *Lonicera* × *grata* is one of the best of the scented kinds, blooming over an exceptionally long period with gentle coloured flowers of soft pinky claret lined with cream which deepens to gold. The late Dutch honeysuckle *L. periclymenum* 'Serotina' is useful with similar but rather deeper coloured flowers and good scent. It flowers in two heavy bursts, in July and September. *L. etrusca* is attractive, particularly when its creamy-yellow flowers are seen against a dark background. This, however, is one of those plants which need patience as it does not flower when young.

Honeysuckles without scent seem a contradiction in terms, nevertheless, there are two species and one hybrid which are generally hardy in this country and whose flowers are of such magnificence that they must not be overlooked here. They are

L. brownii 'Fuchsoides' the large-flowered scarlet trumpet honey-suckle, *L. tragophylla* with three- to four-inch-long flowers of a bright golden-yellow and handsome leaves, and *L.* × *tellmanniana* which also has large leaves and smaller, but still large, flowers of rich yellow tipped with red. The scarlet trumpet honeysuckle flowers both early and late while the other two are midsummer flowers, blooming throughout June and July.

A self-clinging climber to cover the side of a house or an old forest tree is *Schizophragma hydrangeoides*. This carries in July conspicuous flower-heads like those of the lacecap hydrangeas with greeny fertile flowers in the middle and showy, yellow-sepalled outer florets. *S. integrifolium* is even more handsome with large leaves and flower-heads as much as a foot across. It is, however, more susceptible to damage by wind. Both these species are deciduous. There is also a climbing 'hydrangea' which is ever-green—*Pileostegia viburnoides*—which needs a south-west or west wall, or it will ramble over a tree-stump in a sheltered spot. The creamy-white flower-heads appear in autumn.

The passion flower is an old-fashioned climber, needing a west or south-facing wall. *Passiflora caerulea* in the type form is to my mind the most appealing, its ring of blue stamens and darker centre standing out well against the greenish white of the petals. There is an ivory-white form *P. c.* 'Constance Elliott' which I do not think nearly so attractive, and for exceptionally warm and sheltered spots there is a remarkable hybrid raised at Cambridge between 'Constance Elliott' and the exotic *P. quadrangularis*. This is known as *P. allardii* and has its white petals flushed with pink and a deep cobalt-blue corona.

Against a west wall in a mild locality *Solanum crispum* 'Glasnevin' (Glasnevin variety) will do well. This is more of a wall shrub than a climber and its slender growth will sometimes be cut back by frost but will shoot up again in spring. A member of the potato family with similar, curiously shaped flowers in lavender and gold this solanum is most pleasing and an established plant will make a fine show in summer and on into autumn.

I mentioned the winter jasmine in an earlier chapter but the beautifully scented, white, summer jasmine, *Jasminum officinale*, is a twiner which should not be forgotten. It will cover either a porch or a trellis, or would be very pretty rambling through an old holly bush or similar evergreen. Even finer is its variety *J. o.* 'Affine' with larger flowers which are pink on the outside.

For milder districts—we grow them well enough on a south or west wall just over a mile from the sea in North Wales—there are two lovely species: *J. primulinum* and *J. polyanthum*. *J. primulinum* has flowers of the same yellow as the winter jasmine but much larger and usually semi-double in shape. Unfortunately like *J. nudiflorum* it has no scent but, with us at any rate, it is evergreen and so makes an attractive wall furnishing even when out of flower. *J. polyanthum* is the more tender of the two but worth trying in a maritime district. It too is evergreen and has sweetly scented white flowers, borne in panicles, which are pink on the outside. Both these species flower in spring. *J. stephanense* is hardy, will climb to a good height and bears in summer rather small but very fragrant, pale pink flowers.

Invaluable for autumn colour are the vines. For a house wall the true Virginian creeper, *Parthenocissus quinquefolia*, self-clinging, has leaves divided into five leaflets which are bright green in summer and in autumn turn to orange and scarlet. The plant more usually known as 'Virginian creeper' is in fact *Vitis inconstans (Ampelopsis veitchii)*. I do not think it is as handsome in summer as *P. quinquefolia* but its autumn colour is of unsurpassed brilliance. Most striking of all is *V. coignetiae* which has leaves of as much as a foot across, colouring in autumn to a burning orange and crimson.

A delightful shrub *Carpenteria californica*, is not fully hardy but is well worth growing in a warm sunny corner, backed by a wall.

Various new large-flowered clematis hybrids have been introduced; one of the most generally satisfactory is the dusky pink 'Hagley Hybrid'. Several new striped varieties have appeared which in the first flush of publicity bid to outstrip 'Nelly Moser'. None of them so far have proved reliable 'doers', succumbing to wilt or being weak growers. So in this category 'Nelly Moser' must still be first choice.

19

Soil, Cultivation, and Hardiness

Flowering shrubs and trees like any other plants are the better for being grown in good soil. Lime-hating shrubs such as heaths, rhododendrons, pieris, and kalmias have special soil requirements which have been discussed in earlier chapters and which will be mentioned again later in this chapter. Most other shrubs do best in a medium loam that is either neutral or slightly acid in character. However good the loam it will be improved by the incorporation of moisture-holding humus in the form of compost, leaf-mould, peat, rotted manure—or even old newspapers dug in and allowed to rot down.

Where there is a depth of good loam—dark in colour and of good texture—the ground should be trenched before planting. The first trench should be dug two spits deep, the bottom spit being broken up with the fork while the soil from the top spit is barrowed to the other end of the proposed shrub bed or border. The soil dug out of the second trench is then placed in the first trench, the soil from the third trench being placed in the second, and so on as the work proceeds until finally the soil from the first trench is used to fill in the last of the excavations.

Needless to say, during the digging, all weeds should be removed and burnt. It is the thorough initial preparation of the ground which renders a shrub garden comparatively trouble-free when established.

Sometimes there is only a foot or less of good soil overlying a clayey or shaly sub-soil and here it is imperative not to bring the sub-soil to the surface. The sub-soil should be broken up with the fork; at the same time plenty of humus should be incorporated before the top-soil, enriched in its turn with rotted bracken, peat, or leaf-mould is put back, Great care must be taken not to mix the valuable top spit of soil with the poor lower strata.

Apart from that elusive ideal—medium loam—soils fall into two main divisions. They are either light in texture or heavy. Light soils may be sandy or gravelly and while suitable for some of the heaths, dwarf brooms, helianthemums, and other small, spreading shrubs, they need more 'body' and humus before the main run of shrubs will thrive. Such soils desperately need organic matter. Rotted, strawy cow-manure is ideal if you can get it, while hop-manure, lawn-mowings, and sea-weed also are good and may be used with peat, leaf-mould, and compost. Sandy soils are usually deficient in plant foods, so bone-meal, hoof-and-horn, even feathers and leather-dust should be used to provide nourishment, while dressings of bonfire-ash will help to build up the potash content. Superphosphate of lime may be used without fear of its affecting the alkaline content of the soil. I am always wary of using lime in any other form as most shrubs and trees (with the exception of the lilac, prunus, viburnum, and syringa families) and even roses seem to do better in slightly acid soils.

Clay soils are sticky and heavy—yet, if these drawbacks are offset, they are fertile. Their texture may be improved by the addition of sharp sand, fine gravel, rotted horse-manure, compost, leaf-mould, peat, bone-meal, and wood-ash. Clay soils are more troublesome to work when wet or during very hot dry weather. Ridging and leaving the soil broken up through the winter before planting in the spring is of great help. One section of our garden is on a lower stratum than the rest and this part consists of clay which is fortunately covered by eighteen inches of loam elsewhere. When we made the garden we roughly dug the ground in the early autumn, burning all perennial weeds and picking out the worst lumps of clay which we burnt on the garden bonfire. The ground was left broken for the frost and wind to work upon until spring when we dug in, together with the burnt clay from the bonfire, all the organic material available. This section is now one of the most fertile in the garden.

Burnt clay is one of the best of all materials for incorporating in clay soils. Large quantities may be prepared by building a slow-burning garden fire and plastering the clay over it leaving holes at the bottom for ventilation and a smoke shaft at the top. Such a fire will keep in for weeks. When the clay is burned it should be spread out to cool before being dug into the garden when it will greatly improve both the texture and fertility of the soil.

Where the sub-soil is clay, even though the top-soil may be gravel or loam, waterlogging may occur. In such places drainage is essential because few roots will live in waterlogged soil. Drainage pipes are expensive these days so, as an alternative, a trench may be dug two feet deep from the waterlogged area leading to a culvert or ditch where candelabra primulas, and moisture-loving irises will thrive, or even to a garden pool into which the excess moisture may drain. A four-inch layer of stones or clinkers should be placed at the bottom of the trench before the soil is replaced.

Shrubs and trees fall into three categories: those which, like rhododendrons, cannot live in untreated alkaline soils; the great body of shrubs which are lime-tolerant, and those which, like the viburnums and lilacs, seem to prefer an alkaline soil.

Some districts in Britain overlie chalk or limestone strata and here it is better to choose mainly those shrubs and trees which are lime-loving or at any rate lime-tolerant. Such shrubs will grow even in pure chalk provided the chalk is well broken up with a pick-axe before planting so that it provides a deep, moisture-retentive root-run. In some western districts where the rainfall is high there is a layer of acid soil composed of decaying vegetation over limestone. Here, particularly when, as in the coastal belt of North Wales where we live, the water-supply comes from a peaty mountain reservoir away from the limestone it is possible with certain precautions to grow lime-haters. It is up to the individual gardener to decide whether the trouble entailed is worth while and in limestone districts he may decide to avoid altogether the great Ericaceae family or to grow only one or two specimens to which he will be able to give special attention. Generally speaking camellias, clethras, pieris, and the azalea section of the rhododendron genus are the easiest to accommodate by taking out a hole two feet square for each plant and filling it with acid soil. Regular mulching with bracken and rhododendron peat will keep up the acidity and the roots will find their way up into the mulch for moisture and nourishment instead of penetrating into the alkaline soil below. Care must be taken to water only with rain-water, avoiding piped water where it is known to contain lime. Not all limestone areas, however, have lime in the water. It may be drawn from some peaty, mountain reservoir in which case it will do the plants no harm.

The acidity or alkalinity of soil is measured by a pH scale, and those of a scientific turn of mind may like to know that pH is a measure of hydrogen-ion concentration. A pH of 7·0 is the neutral point where acidity and alkalinity are in the balance. A pH of 7·5 is alkaline and the alkalinity increases as pH 8·0, pH 8·5, etc., are reached. On the other hand pH 6·5 is on the acid side of neutral. A pH of 5·3 is considered ideal for rhododendrons while below 4·5 is too acid, and bone-meal (which, as bones are mainly calcium in content, is naturally alkaline) should be added to sweeten the soil.

Where the pH is 7·0 or below but above 5·3 the acidity needs to be increased if rhododendrons, kalmias, pieris, embothriums, camellias, etc., are to be at their best. Some herbaceous plants, notably the meconopses, Asiatic primulas and Asiatic gentians, and Japanese irises need an acid soil.

Neutral and insufficiently acid soils may be made more acid by the use of bracken and rhododendron peat. Leaf-mould, as stated earlier, is usually alkaline in content and so is more suitable for lime-tolerant and lime-loving genera than for the lime-haters. Flowers of sulphur may be used to increase acidity. When planting calcifuge plants on alkaline soil it is a wise precaution to line the planting-holes with flowers of sulphur before filling with acid soil. Should chlorosis (inter-veinal yellowing of the foliage) appear the plant should be treated with iron Sequestrene.

Soil may be roughly judged by the type of vegetation found wild in a district. Where heather and bracken thrive, the top-soil, at any rate, is acid. Old man's beard, traveller's joy, and yew on the other hand indicate alkalinity. The shrub gardener, however, needs more exact guidance than this. A soil-testing apparatus is marketed by British Drug Houses. Currently available at a reasonable price it will enable you to take samples of soils from various parts of your garden and test whether the reaction is acid or alkaline. Although it indicates degrees of acidity (in colours each of which may be interpreted as being equivalent to 0·5 degrees of the pH scale) it does not indicate the varying degrees of alkalinity and —having apparently been devised primarily for vegetable-growers— shows the relative degrees of acidity in the terms of lime needed. Except in the case of known lime-loving plants the shrub gardener would do well to ignore its advice regarding liming and to be grateful for any assurance it may give as to the acidity of his soil.

If, however, your soil is very acid, pH 5·5 or below, and you wish, like most of us, to grow viburnums, lilacs, flowering cherries, clematis, and such lime-loving plants it is wise to establish them in separate beds away from the lime-haters, to dig in leaf-mould and bone-meal at the rate of six ounces to the square yard, and to dress the bed yearly with ground limestone.

Mulching is a most important part of shrub-garden routine. We use bracken, chopped green in June, and mulch again in spring when the soil has begun to warm, with compost. Fallen leaves are left beneath the shrubs where they fall and this generous natural mulch is reinforced each autumn by collected leaves from the lawn and paths and an occasional sackful of leaves for the non-calcifuge plants, or pine-needles for the calcifuge, from the near-by woods. Rotted bracken scooped from beneath the brown fronds in winter is a valuable additional mulching material that is especially valuable for the lime-haters.

At first thought, chopping the bracken for the summer mulch may seem to present some problems. We have found that small quantities may be easily cut and roughly chopped with long-handled shears. For larger quantities quite the most satisfactory method is to put the bracken though a chaff-cutter which in country districts may be bought reasonably cheaply at the sale of some outgoing farm-tenant.

Bracken cut in June is rich in the potash which many lime-hating plants seem to lack. Wood-ash which might be used to supply potash to the non-calcifuge is death to many calcifuge plants but bracken is not only a safe source of supply but applied as a mulch, helps to retain soil moisture and to smother weed growth. It is important to cut the bracken early before the spores are ripe otherwise the ripe spores might result in an infestation of bracken in the garden.

Compost from the garden heap is a valuable mulch for the shrub garden. We never use it on rhododendrons which get all the nutriment they need from chopped green bracken and peat (with perhaps the aforementioned additional mulch of rotted bracken in winter) but camellias and magnolias benefit from the compost as will roses, viburnums, lilacs, and almost every other genus of shrubs and trees.

The compost-heap should stand directly on the soil, preferably in a shallow trench and should be built in sandwich-like layers. Plant-remains, grass-clippings, sea-weed, vegetable-waste from the kitchen, tea-leaves, rags, sawdust, the contents of the vacuum-bag are all suitable for composting. Start with a layer of coarse material (not woody stems which should always be burned) eight to twelve inches thick and cover this with a two-inch layer of soil. Then add a sprinkling of dried poultry-guano or fish-manure to activate the material and help it to rot. Add a twelve-inch layer of finer material such as grass-clippings; then more soil and more guano, continuing in this order until a sizeable heap is made and covered with soil. The heap should be kept moist as it is built. After ten weeks it should be turned and after six months it should be ready to use. It will, however, be better if left for a full twelve months. Good compost is dark, moist, crumbly like cake, and sweet-smelling. A good gardener will have two or three heaps—one for use, one maturing, and one in the process of being built. The ground occupied is in no sense wasted and may be screened from view by wattles or a hedge of *Berberis darwinii* or other small evergreen.

Mulching does away with the need for hoeing and for that regrettable forking so beloved of jobbing gardeners which leads to the death of choice underplantings and bulbs, sometimes to the death of the shrubs themselves and prevents the self-sown spread and naturalizing of desirable plants. Used on its own or in conjunction with vigorous herbaceous underplanting, the mulch does away with much of the need for weeding. Any weeds which appear in it are easily picked out by hand and a four- to six-inch mulch effectively suffocates most weeds in the soil beneath. It also suppresses any choice seedlings one might wish to cherish so, in areas which one wants to colonize with woodland plants or bulbs, the mulch should be kept to a two-inch maximum. By mulching, the labour of maintenance in the small shrub garden can be cut to a minimum. Mulches should not be applied when the ground is dry as they would act as a blanket and keep out the rain. It is wisest to mulch after a heavy shower or after the area in question has been thoroughly soaked with the hose.

The mulch should not be forked in. Rhododendrons and surface-rooting shrubs like to send their roots up into the mulch. Where this does not happen, worms and weather will eventually carry the mulching material beneath the surface—but long before that it will be time to mulch again. Nothing is more beneficial to shrubs and trees than regular mulching with the right material—nor is anything more labour-saving.

Frost is a garden menace, however, against which even mulching gives only slight protection. How heartbreaking it is to the keen gardener to cherish a slightly tender shrub for years only to lose it by severe frost when it is of a size to leave a considerable gap in the garden planting. Hardiness seems to vary from garden to garden. I have seen ceanothus bushes killed by frost in gardens on one side of the road while those on the other have escaped with no more than a light searing of their leaves.

Air-drainage has a great bearing on the problem. Frost will drain from a hillside garden to linger, with serious consequences, in the garden in a valley. Yet even a hillside garden may suffer severe frost damage if the air-drainage is blocked by a high wall or a thick planting of evergreens. On the other hand an evergreen-screen may be planted to block the path of ice-bearing winds and so to benefit considerably any tender plants in its lee.

Some shrubs flower in mid-winter, and their blossoms seem

unharmed by heavy frost. Such is the Chinese witch hazel, *Hamamelis mollis. Rhododendron mucronulatum*, flowering at the same time, has blossoms that are definitely frost-tender. To enjoy the complementary planting of both witch-hazel and rhododendron, the shrubs should be sited on the north of a large bush such as a well-grown holly or *R. ponticum* or on the north of a wall or wattle fence where the morning sun will not strike the frosted blooms. An overhead canopy of deciduous trees will help to protect the blooms. At Bodnant, a magnificent bush of *R. mucronulatum* blooms unperturbed through quite severe frost, its blossoms saved by the dense, woodland shelter of the trees and bushes among which it is planted. Only the flowers of the rhododendron are susceptible to frost. Cistuses on the other hand are definitely tender. In some gardens frost kills them outright. Yet in others they survive zero frosts. Here, I think, the answer lies in soil drainage combined with sufficient summer sunshine thoroughly to ripen the wood. Grown on a shaly, steeply sloping, sun-baked bank in poor soil, cistuses seem unbelievably hardy. Such conditions approximate to those in their natural habitat, where winter frosts are not unknown. Generally speaking, exposure to sun and wind helps to harden all small-leafed shrubs.

The evergreen ceanothuses, with their blue thimbles of spring and summer bloom, revel in such a site. If their roots are anchored with stones to prevent wind-rock, they will prove hardier on an exposed bank than in their more generally chosen position against a house or garden wall.

Some of the small-leafed dwarf rhododendrons are early flowering by nature but an exposed site will retard their flowering, perhaps until the frost is over; it will also make them hardier. It is necessary to emphasize that only the small-leafed section must be treated in this way. Larger-leafed shrubs suffer loss of moisture by the exposure of their greater leaf-surfaces to wind and so may die as much from this cause as from the frost against which we are trying to harden them.

Winter damp is often as great a danger as frost; this is why soil drainage must always be good. Plants which need a great deal of moisture should have retentive humus incorporated in the soil in the form of peat, leaf-mould, or rotted bracken and in heavy soils a layer of chippings may be used to cover the bottom of the planting-hole. This will help to aerate a heavy soil and so combat the harmful effect on shrub roots of standing in cold, stagnant water.

Anyone who has set their heart on growing rhododendrons, camellias and other shallow-rooted calcifuges in alkaline soils may find a reasonably sure method of success if they excavate a shallow depression, perhaps eighteen inches deep, lining it with heavy-duty black polythene and, using this as a base, build up a raised bed of acid soil (pH 5 is best) bounded by sandstone or granite rock or peat walls.

The bed must be above the level of the surrounding soil so that calcium cannot seep in and it should slope from back to front to allow any surplus moisture to drain away.

An acid grade of coarse peat or acid-reacting loam mixed with leaf-mould from woodland on acid ground, or well-rotted bracken, would be the ideal growing medium and a surface mulch of chopped green bracken in June would ensure the shrubs rooting upwards into the mulch and away from the lime.

20

Planting, Staking, Watering

From November to March is generally recommended as the planting-time for leaf-losing trees and shrubs while September and October, or April and May are often recommended for evergreens. In many districts the ground is too dry in most years to move anything—either evergreen or deciduous—until the end of October, while, with us, March and April are usually times of spring drought. So one must compromise. I should say that it is safe to move evergreens at any time during the winter months. With bought-in stock, however, the generally preferred planting-time is November. This means that nurserymen are then kept busy, so busy in fact that anyone who has not given an order in good time has to take his place well down the queue of garden owners awaiting plant deliveries and may not receive his plants until January!

To be sure of getting one's plants early in November the order must reach the nurseryman by August at the latest. If this is neglected and the plants are not delivered until well on into the winter there is no need to feel disheartened. Plant as soon as the bundles arrive, if at all possible. If the ground is frozen too hard to make a good job of the planting, break the soil—with a pick-axe if necessary—and heel the shrubs in, taking them out of their wrappings but being careful to keep any root-balls intact, and putting the plants in a trench at an angle and well covered with soil. Should the ground be too hard to break even with a pick-axe, then you will have to leave the plants as they are, in their wrappings, and store them in a cool but frost-proof place until the thaw. I would stress, though, that it is better, if at all possible, to find some spot in which to heel in the plants; the ground beneath the compost-heap is usually soft and in an emergency the heap should be drawn to one side and the plants heeled into the soft ground thus exposed. If you are working all week and the plants are waiting when you get home from the office, heel them in by the aid of your car head-lights if necessary, and they will suffer no harm until you are able to plant them at the week-end.

Should the roots seem dry, it is helpful to soak them in water for six hours or even more before planting. Bare-rooted trees should in any case have their roots puddled in a bucket of wet mud for half an hour before planting.

Choice plants such as magnolias, rhododendrons, kalmias, and all conifers will arrive with their roots balled in sacking. I usually remove the sacking though some gardeners merely untie and slacken it, pulling it well away at the top. Whichever method you follow it is essential not to disturb the root-ball which should be planted intact.

Planting-holes are sometimes dug in advance for special reasons —if, for instance, spring planting is to be carried out on clay soils. As a rule, however, it is better to dig the hole at the time of planting. Previously, of course, the site, if not the whole border, will have been dug over and well-laced with humus. So at planting-time it will be easy to take out the required hole which should be big enough comfortably to take the spread-out roots of the tree or shrub.

The planting-hole should always be twice as wide as necessary so that when the roots begin to grow they can thrust easily into the crumbly tilth of the prepared site instead of meeting the resistance of uncultivated ground. Although the hole should err on the side of being too wide rather than too cramped, never let it be too deep. Try to plant so that the tree or shrub is at the exact depth (shown by the soil-mark on the stem) at which it grew in the nursery from which it came. Mound a little soil in the centre of the hole on which the plant can 'sit' as it were, and gently spread out the roots all round. I like to mix peat with the soil to crumble over the roots, as this helps to give them a start. Trample

17. The shapely lacecap flower heads of *Hydrangea* 'Mariesii'

18. *Itea ilicifolia* is charming in late summer when it bears long, fragrant catkins of greeny-white flowers

19. *Magnolia stellata* takes up little space

20. Pernettya berries in lilac, pink, maroon and white give welcome colour in the autumn garden

21. *Philadelphus* 'Innocence' often has creamy-white variegations in the leaves. It is one of the best of the single-flowered mock oranges

22. *Prunus* 'Mikuruma-gaeshi' is a shapely and free-flowering tree for a limited space

23. *Pyracantha atalantoides* 'Aurea', a yellow-berried pyracantha which is especially useful in that—in common with those of most yellow-fruited shrubs—its berries tend to be left alone by the birds

24. The fringed dianthus-like flowers of *Rosa rugosa* 'Pink Grootendorst' are borne on a bush that with us is free-flowering and vigorous

the soil down as you fill in the hole but be careful not to leave the top-soil packed hard. After firming, it should be gently loosened with the rake.

In the case of deciduous trees, a stake will be necessary to prevent wind-rock and this should be put into the ground in the planting-hole before the tree. Sometimes it is possible to drive a sharpened stake into the earth for the necessary eighteen inches or two feet but more often one has to take out a deep hole with the trowel, putting in the stake, wedging it with stones and ramming it firmly into the ground before the tree is planted.

The stake should, before planting, have been treated with some wood preservative (of the kind sold for horticultural use and guaranteed harmless to plants).

All gardens have their prevailing wind—usually from the south-west—so the stake should be placed between the tree and the prevailing wind and securely fastened with a suitable tie. There are many proprietary tree-ties on the market and most of them are good. If you do not want to go to the expense of buying special ties, adequate ones may be made from lengths of broad, plastic clothes-line crossed to form a figure-of-eight round the stake and round the tree. Or you may use a rope or wire running through a length of hose-pipe. The important thing is to prevent the bark being rubbed, and to this end some gardeners fasten a collar of canvas or sacking round the tree before making the tie. With plastic line or hose-pipe, however, this is unnecessary. When a fixed tie is used the tree must be examined fairly frequently as the tie needs to be slackened as the tree grows. Failure to attend to this restricts the flow of sap and often results in unsightly ridges on the trunks of trees and may eventually lead to the death of the tree.

Sometimes it is possible to tell which way the tree has been growing in the nursery (moss on the bark generally indicates the north) and when this is the case I always try to plant it facing the same way. However, if the tree appears to have been blown by the wind in one direction it is as well to plant it the other way round so that the growth may have a chance to right itself. Occasionally one gets shrubs or trees, usually evergreens, the shape of which has been spoiled by growing in too close proximity to nursery neighbours. Plenty of light and air around such a shrub in its new site will usually correct this, but if one side is poor and thin I try to place that side to the south so that the sunlight may encourage new growth to break. Spraying the foliage of such trees or shrubs with water in spring will also help to put matters right.

During the first spring and summer after planting many shrubs and trees are particularly susceptible to drought. This is especially true of the fleshy-rooted magnolias in whose case spring planting is often recommended in cold districts. Particular attention should be paid to such spring-planted shrubs, watering frequently during dry spells. If drying winds occur after the leaves have appeared it is helpful to erect a screen of hessian or sacking to protect the foliage and so avoid that excess loss of moisture, via the leaves, which would weaken the plant. Many evergreen plants, particularly medium- and large-leafed rhododendrons and the various conifers, will also benefit from such an arrangement. They will also appreciate having their foliage sprayed during spells when drying winds prevail. In winter, tepid water should be used and sprayed on to the plants with an ordinary garden syringe. During spring and summer droughts when many evergreens need such attention I have found it quite satisfactory to spray with ordinary mains water via the nozzle of the hose-pipe although this of course should not be resorted to when dealing with lime-haters in areas where the tap-water is limy.

Experiments recently carried out seem to show that frequent foliage spraying during hot weather is of even more benefit than weekly soakings of the soil. Established plants that have been well mulched when the ground is moist should not need watering except during prolonged drought although, even in such cases, foliage spraying of evergreens will be beneficial if you have the time to do it. 'Keep the hoe going' is a maxim which should certainly *never* be followed in the shrub garden. Hoeing harms the roots of shrubs, destroys valuable seedlings, and possibly even helps the soil to dry out. Mulching is in every way more satisfactory.

21

Pruning

Nothing can spoil the appearance of a shrub more than wrong pruning. Most gardeners seem to prune too much. One sees flowering cherries ruthlessly beheaded, lilacs pruned to an unhappy stick with a tuft of flowers at the end, forsythia and flowering currant clipped to box-like shapes—a luckless travesty of their carefree selves. No sight is more pathetic, and yet such crimes are usually committed in the name of keen gardening.

Pruning is often undertaken at the wrong time. One sees escallonias clipped in May so that the June crop of flowers is lost. It is a safe general rule to prune as soon as the flowers are over. With the exception of heaths and broom, which should be sheared after flowering (without cutting back into the old wood), most shrubs (other than those grown in hedges) should not be touched with the shears. Such clipping usually results in excessive growth and the loss of flowers. Far better to prune by removing old shoots from the base with saw or secateurs. Most strong-growing shrubs may have all the four-year-old stems removed without loss of flower. If treated in this way they will keep their natural shape and will not become too big for their positions.

It is customary to prune buddleias in March, cutting right back into the hardwood. This serves very well the purpose of the gardener with limited space. It results in moderate-sized bushes with many wands of flower. On the other hand, against a wall or in a sheltered corner buddleias pruned only lightly will grow into graceful trees. Sometimes, against a house, specimens pruned in this way will reach twenty feet and produce a succession of flower-

163

heads in mauve, purple, reddish-purple, or white over a long period.

Shrub roses, as I outlined in the appropriate chapter, should have their dead or weak wood cut out while a longer succession of flowers will result if the side-shoots are shortened by a third to a convenient bud. This is best done in winter. Climbing roses should have an occasional strong shoot cut back to provide flower at a lower level. It is not within my province here to deal with the pruning of hybrid tea roses. I can do no better than to recommend readers interested to consult Mr. F. Fairbrother's excellent *Roses* published by Penguin Books in conjunction with the Royal Horticultural Society.

Clematis are among the most useful and colourful climbers for the shrub garden. The species should not as a rule be pruned, except to restrain over-vigorous and tangled growth in the case of *Clematis montana*, its rose coloured variety *C. m.* 'Rubens', and the allied *C. chrysocoma*. Hybrids of the *C. patens* and *C. lanuginosa* type, such as the well-known 'Nelly Moser', 'William E. Gladstone', 'Lasurstern', and 'Prince Hendrick' are best left unpruned. Strong-growers of the *C. jackmannii* and *C. viticella* section such as 'Comtesse de Bouchaud', 'Ville de Lyon', and 'Lady Northcliffe' may have the previous year's wood cut to a foot of its base (the shoot's base, not the plant's!) but they may equally well be left unpruned and provided they are given a little guidance, by gentle training of their tendrils in the way they should go, clematis treated in this way seem even freer flowering and certainly cover more space than hard-pruned plants.

Care must be taken not to leave snags of branches or twigs when pruning. Not only are these unsightly but they will often be the start of die-back or rot. I have seen a lovely old magnolia become the victim of careless pruning. A branch broken by wind was crudely cut back leaving a stump, rain collected in the axil of the stump and a soft rot set in, affecting the trunk so that the only remedy was to cut out the whole stem. When branches have to be removed from established trees the cut should be made with a sharp saw, flush with the main trunk so far as possible. The wound should then be trimmed with the knife until it is quite smooth and there are no projecting pieces. 'Stockholm tar' may be painted over the wound except in the case of magnolias which seem allergic to the tar. Instead use a paint that contains no lead. Lead-containing paint should not be used to seal a wound.

When pruning it is as well to look ahead and remove awkwardly placed branches while they are still slender enough to be cut with the secateurs or knife. Ornamental cherries are apt to bleed when cut, so in their case one must be particularly far-sighted and pinch out those growth-buds that seem likely to result in unwanted wood. Generally speaking, there should be no need to prune such subjects unless as sometimes happens a branch is likely to grow across a path or to shade unduly a neighbouring shrub.

Grafted subjects—shrubs and trees in which a choice variety has been grafted upon a common stock such as the ornamental cherries, crab-apples, lilacs, azaleas, roses, rhododendrons, witch hazels, etc.—must be closely watched for the appearance of suckers. In such cases any shoots appearing from below the graft or below the soil must be cut out. Chopping them back with a spade only results in more and stronger suckers. Lay bare the base of the sucker with the trowel, trace it back to its origin on the parent stock and remove it cleanly with a knife.

Nowadays it is possible to buy from the specialist nurseries rhododendrons and azaleas upon their own roots and this I always try to do, as grafted plants of this order may cause endless annoyance and if the suckers are neglected the stock may take over and choke out the choice scion. Lilacs too should be purchased on their own roots wherever possible. Even when this is the case all suckers should be removed as too much sucker-growth uses up the strength which would otherwise be spent in flowering. Plants flower in order to attract insects to fertilize for fruit. When they are propagating themselves in other ways—by suckers, etc.— they have no need to flower and so unchecked sucker-growth leads to poor flowering.

Ornamental cherries and other members of the prunus family in which the graft is often from four to six inches above ground should be closely watched in spring and early summer for the appearance of any shoots below the graft which can be clearly seen. If caught early it is a simple matter with finger and thumb to 'rub out' the unwanted growth.

Like lilac, *Viburnum farreri* is apt to sucker freely from the base. These suckers should be severely limited. The surplus young shoots may be detached and grown on in a nursery bed either to increase one's own stock or to provide welcome gifts for friends.

The time of pruning varies according to the flowering-time of the plant. Forsythias, *Kerria japonica*, brooms, etc., which flower in the spring should be pruned immediately after flowering. In fact the general rule is to prune as soon as the flowers are over except in the case of certain tender subjects which flower in late summer (hydrangeas, buddleias, etc.), which should have the old growth left for winter protection, being pruned in spring only when frost danger has passed.

Chaenomeles (cydonias)—both when grown in the open and against a wall—should be spur-pruned in the fashion of fruit trees, side-shoots being cut back to two or three buds from the base in November to encourage the formation of flower-buds. If this is not done they tend to make rampant thorny growth which takes off from the effectiveness of the flowers.

Except when a shoot is to be cut right out to the ground (and here again care should be taken not to leave any protruding snag) growth should always be pruned back to a bud, the cut being made with a downward slant away from the bud. To cut towards the bud might result in water lodging in the axil of the bud and causing it to rot.

Many shrubs including camellias, rhododendrons, azaleas, kalmias, *Garrya elliptica*, hamamelis, etc., really need no pruning unless they are outgrowing their space. Rhododendrons that have become leggy may be cut back to improve their shape, otherwise this section is unlikely to need pruning at all. We always cut out unwanted shoots, or branches which overshadow their neighbours, when in flower so that one may have the advantage of the blooms indoors.

Some people like to grow the scarlet barked dogwood *Cornus alba* 'Sibirica' (of which the Westonbirt variety is the best) and the yellow and orange barked willows for the beauty of their coloured stems in winter. To encourage the production of the most brilliant stems and to keep the plants within bounds the plants should be cut back to within nine inches of the ground in early spring.

In the small garden it is important to keep shrubs within bounds and to prevent them encroaching on one another. If this happens, their shape is usually spoiled. One or the other will become bare at the base or may even weaken and die.

By going round the garden frequently, with a watchful eye, potential trouble can often be spotted and the offending branch cut out to be used for decoration indoors or consigned to the bonfire.

In spring, when the shoots extend, one can often see the necessity to nip back shoots that threaten to become over-long. If the wood has hardened, secateurs must be used, but when the growth is sappy it can usually be 'pinched out' between finger and thumb.

Growth thus shortened in May often leads to fresh shoots being made, so one must go round again in July to repeat the process.

22

Propagation

Most keen gardeners find the propagation of their stock rewarding, and where herbaceous underplanting and shrubs are concerned it can be both money-saving and reasonably quick. Many bulbs unfortunately take so long to flower that few of us have the patience to undertake raising them from seed. It pays, however, to leave seed-pods on snowdrops, crocus species, dwarf daffodils, cyclamen, and dog's tooth violets and to avoid disturbing the soil around them, picking out all weeds by hand, and forswearing the hoe. Where this practice is followed, seedlings will readily appear and although they may take from three to five years or more to flower they will often result in the successful establishment of wide colonies of bulbs. A similar practice may well be followed with herbaceous underplantings which are usually quicker to bloom from seed. Primula species increase readily in this way and will usually flower in their second year. Hellebores usually take three years to flower. Aquilegias, foxgloves, campanulas, pulmonarias, etc., can usually be relied upon for self-increase. *Meconopsis betonicifolia* needs to be specially sown (under glass in February, has been found the most successful). It should not be allowed to flower in its second year as plants flowering before the formation of their second basal rosette generally die. Any premature flower-stems should be pinched out from the base directly they appear. It should be said, however, that even this measure does not always succeed. Some plants of this species seem naturally monocarpic and whereas seventy-five per cent of the plants will wait naturally to form sturdy subsidiary rosettes before flowering, the odd twenty-five per cent may die whether disbudded or not. Some gardeners, therefore, prefer to let nature take its course and to enjoy the flowers as they come.

Many dwarf shrubs like the mountain rhododendrons, the evergreen azaleas, shrubby blue flax, hypericums, lavender, helianthemums, etc., come freely from seed although naturally they take longer to make large plants than do the herbaceous subjects. Dwarf rhododendrons in particular flower at a very early age and are well worth raising from seed. It should be understood, however, that only the species, whether of shrubby or herbaceous subjects, will come true from seed, and that hybrids cannot be relied upon to reproduce themselves accurately.

As a general rule it pays to sow perennial seeds and the seeds of shrubs and trees in pots or pans in a greenhouse or cold frame. The utensils should always be scrupulously clean and the compost sterilized otherwise the seedlings may suffer from the disease known as 'damping off'. Specially prepared 'John Innes Seed Compost' can be bought from most nurserymen and from the seed-shops and is satisfactory for the propagation of all plants except the lime-haters. This standard compost contains chalk and so is unsuitable for rhododendrons, azaleas, kalmias, heaths, pieris, Asiatic gentians, gaultherias, and all known calcifuge plants. For these it is wisest to make up one's own seed compost of two parts sterilized acid turf loam, one part of peat, and one part coarse sand. To this may be added one and a half ounces of superphosphate per bushel of compost.

The loam may be sterilized as described in potting and composting books. To save trouble you may prefer to do as I do and buy sterilized, prepared loam from your local nurseryman.

It is essential that the pots should have a thick layer of crocks or weathered, sifted ashes at the bottom to help drainage. The drainage material should be covered with half-decayed leaves or—better, in the case of lime-haters, at any rate—with sphagnum moss. The pot should then be filled with compost to within a quarter of an inch of the top, tamping down the surface so that it is firm but not hard. Then the pot should be stood in water which does not quite reach the top until the compost is thoroughly moist.

PROPAGATION

Sow the seeds thinly and cover them lightly with compost. The depth of the soil should be roughly as deep as the diameter of the seeds. Very fine seeds such as those of rhododendrons and azaleas need only a light dusting with sand to anchor them. I always use fine grit to lightly cover the surface after sowing and this seems to assist germination and to allow overhead watering without it causing the packing down and hardening of the soil surface.

After sowing, the pots should be covered with a pane of glass to prevent evaporation and shaded with paper against the sun. Alternatively a Polythene bag may be placed over the top and supported by crossing half-hoops of wire or cane to prevent it touching the surface. A rubber ring will secure the Polythene bag below the rim of the pot. The pots may then be brought into a greenhouse or placed in a frame upon a bed of ashes. Over-watering must be avoided but on the other hand the pots should never be allowed to dry out. As soon as the seeds germinate the glass or Polythene covers should be removed.

The seeds of Asiatic and European primulas, most gentians, and almost all high alpine plants germinate more freely if sown in winter and if the pots are stood out of doors under a north-facing wall or hedge. The alternate freezing and thawing approximates to the natural conditions of an alpine habitat and so the seeds will usually germinate readily when brought into a warmer place. On the other hand, the cyclamen-like dodecatheons, willow gentians, the spring-flowering anemone-like adonis, and other choice seeds from lower altitudes germinate better if sown under glass in spring. *Sanguinaria canadensis* and the trilliums take two years to germinate and should be stood out of doors in their pans and left for two winters and summers of alternate frost, thaw and heat for the seedlings to appear. Raising such treasures is not for the impatient gardener but how rewarding it is when at last the seed-leaves push through.

Once the first pair of true leaves (the seed-leaves are cotyledons and do not count for our purpose) appear, the seeds should be pricked out into a nursery bed or into individual pots. Herbaceous plants will usually be ready to plant into their permanent positions

by autumn but shrubs and trees will usually need to remain in
their nursery rows for another season at least.

Many shrubs and trees may be propagated even more quickly by
cuttings. This method of reproduction has the advantage where
hybrids are concerned as cuttings, being the actual wood of the
parent plant, will remain true to type.

Cuttings are of two main types—hardwood and softwood.
Hardwood cuttings consist of a ripened shoot, ten to eighteen
inches long, of the parent plant, taken with a heel in October or
November. I never touch hardwood cuttings with the knife. I
pull the shoots away by hand and insert them for three-quarters of
their length in a narrow slanting trench the bottom of which has
been lined with sand or peat. I like to place my cuttings at a slight
angle and so place them against the slanting side of the trench
before replacing the soil and firming. This method is suitable for
the easier run of coarser shrubs such as forsythias, philadelphuses,
lilacs, flowering currants, willows, etc. Less vigorous subjects—
hypericums and potentillas for example—are more likely to succeed
if nearly ripe shoots are taken in August. July is the month for
taking shrub-rose cuttings, and I have found such ground-covering
subjects as alpine phloxes and helianthemums to strike freely if
inserted in June. *Viburnum* × *burkwoodii*, too, strikes freely at this
time of the year.

So far we have been dealing with open-ground cuttings which
should be inserted in a prepared bed of friable soil mixed with
sand or peat on the north side of a wall or hedge or in a similar
shady spot. Experience will soon enable you to select the right
wood for cuttings. The wood should be reasonably firm and as far
as possible unflowered shoots should be chosen. Sometimes it is
impossible to find an unflowered shoot and then a compromise can
be made by trimming back a flowered shoot to the top leaf or pair
of leaves (there will be a growth-bud in the axil of the leaf) and
removing any flower-buds which may have formed.

Plants so raised should not be disturbed until the autumn of the
following year.

Other shrubs such as the hardy fuchsias, hydrangeas, evergreen
azaleas, jasmines, hebes (veronicas), dwarf rhododendrons,

tricuspidaria, desfontainea, or osmanthus strike best from cuttings of half-ripe wood of recent growth severed below a node and taken in July and inserted .in a closed frame or in Polythene-covered pots. Care must be taken, however, when using Polythene covers, to use only sterilized compost because for some reason the use of Polythene renders the cuttings particularly susceptible to damping off. I lost several batches in this way before I realized the cause of the trouble. Now, with sterile compost, success is at least eighty per cent. The Polythene should be kept well above the cuttings by half-hoops of wire or cane and secured over the rim of the pot with a rubber band. Polythene-covered cuttings seldom need watering (once in fourteen days is an average) but of course a watch must be kept to see that they do not dry out. Nor is there any need to wipe away the condensation from the inside of the Polythene. It falls back into the pot, keeping the soil and cutting moist and encouraging growth. Once growth begins, the Polythene cover should be removed.

Home-made frames can be constructed quite satisfactorily from bottomless boxes so that they slope to the south and are covered with sheets of glass. Having no spare space for large, permanent frames, these are all I ever use. I find them most satisfactory if sited in half-shade and covered with matting during spells of hot sunshine. A compost of fibrous loam and peat seems to give the best results. Leaf-mould should never be used as it encourages damping off. When the cuttings are first inserted, the frame should be kept closed, air being admitted once a day when the condensation is wiped off the glass. Daily watering is essential and in very hot weather I have often had to water twice and even three times a day. When growth begins, more air should be admitted, the frame being propped open for a couple of inches during the day at first and closed at night. Gradually hardening-off is accomplished and the glass is left off entirely. During hard frost, however, I replace the glass and cover with matting to give additional protection. Cuttings raised in this way are usually ready to plant out into a nursery bed in the following April.

Layering is a useful way of obtaining new plants of those genera which do not strike readily from cuttings. A low branch is pulled

PROPAGATION

down to the ground, covered with soil and peat and secured with a wooden peg or covered with soil and peat and weighted down by a heavy stone. Often but by no means always, a tongue-shaped slit is made in the underside of the branch to encourage rooting. Usually it is necessary only to scrape the bark gently with a knife to give a wounded surface which will callus and form roots easily. Root-formation is helped if the branch is bent as acutely as possible so that the tip, which will form the new plant, rises vertically into the air. To ensure this it may be secured to a cane. The time taken for the layered part to form sufficient roots to withstand being severed from the parent plant varies from genus to genus. Dwarf rhododendrons of the 'Blue Tit' type will root in a year or less; so will most heathers and shrubs of the diervilla, forsythia, philadelphus category. Larger rhododendrons, magnolias, acers, etc., are usually ready to be severed from the parent plant in eighteen months to two years. After the new plant has been separated from the parent it should be left *in situ* for a month or two so that its roots become accustomed to the burden of providing its sole nourishment before it is transplanted and they suffer the shock of the removal and have to adjust themselves to a new site.

With the advent of Polythene, the layering process has been speeded up. Air-layering has been made possible for all.

Air-layering was previously a highly specialized art, used in greenhouses on large estates where a constant supply of garden boys was available to moisten the layers, which were encased in sphagnum moss in halved pots. Now, encased in Polythene instead of halved pots, moss keeps the layer moist until the rooting process is completed. Hormone rooting powders, though not essential to the striking of cuttings, make a big difference to the success of air-layering operations. The usual 'L 15' is the formula to choose for most subjects, including the small and medium-leafed rhododendrons, roses, magnolias, and acers other than the Japanese *Acer palmatum*. 'L 30' ensures success with large-leafed rhododendrons and *A. palmatum*, and I prefer to use it for subjects such as the tulip tree, ginko, and others which seem as if they might prove difficult.

The method is simple. A shoot of one-year-old wood as thick as an ordinary pencil is chosen, and a cut two inches long is made up the middle of the stem just under a bud or leaf axil, six inches to twelve inches from the apex of the shoot. With a child's paint-brush, hormone powder is brushed into the cut, which is held well open with a piece of sphagnum moss. (The sphagnum moss is obtained from any florist, moistened with rainwater, and squeezed to remove excess moisture.) Sphagnum moss is wrapped round the layered portion of the stem, and a Polythene tube (a Polythene bag with the end cut off) is slipped over the whole and bound securely in place with insulating-tape at each end. Both ends should be bound by the tape which should start on the Polythene and end on the stem.

Root-formation may be seen through the film, and after sufficient roots are seen to have formed the layer is severed below the lower insulating-tape, and the tape and Polythene are removed together with as much of the moss as is possible without damaging the roots. The portion of stem below the roots is cut off and the new plant is potted ready to be planted out in the following autumn. Some plants will root very quickly by this method; others may take a year or longer. Where failures occur they will usually be found to be attributable to the use of too much hormone (which clogs the surface of the cut and seems to seal it so that the roots cannot emerge), or to failure to wedge the cut properly open— with the result that the wood knits together again, and no roots emerge.

The romneyas are one of the few shrubby subjects propagated by means of root cuttings although this method is common among herbaceous subjects. Border phlox, anchusas, Japanese anemones, globe thistles, Oriental poppies, incarvilleas, gypsophilas, and choice primroses are often increased in this way. Portions of root about three inches long, cut square at the top and sloping at the bottom are inserted upright, and just covered in boxes of sandy soil in a frame. The soil should be kept moist and by the following spring the cuttings will be ready to be planted out.

Grafting and budding are methods of propagation best left in expert hands and in any case I believe that it is more satisfactory to have as many subjects as possible upon their own roots. Even the ornamental cherries and acers which mostly prove intractable to strike from cuttings may now be increased by air-layering.

Nurserymen will still graft cherries and crabs, hamamelis and similar plants which are slow to reach saleable size. It is unlikely that air-layering which is a comparatively slow and rather a painstaking job will ever be largely used in commercial practice. However, mist techniques have increased the possibilities of raising plants in quantity from cuttings and more and more specialist nurserymen are producing rhododendrons and azaleas raised from layers and cuttings and so growing upon their own roots. Perhaps the time is not so far distant when in every practicable case plants may be purchased upon their own roots. The weeping cherries, however, in nature creep along the ground as does *Cotoneaster* 'Hybridus Pendulus', so in cases like these there will always be a necessity for grafting where standard trees are desired.

Some of the new miniature propagators with electrical soil warming equipment can be very useful, enabling a higher percentage of cuttings to strike. They are useful also in the raising of seedlings but attention must always be paid to proper hardening off, otherwise plantlets raised in this way may suddenly collapse without the support of the propagator.

23

Pests and Diseases

Few of the insect pests which attack ornamental shrubs and trees are in themselves serious but they are often unsightly and in any case they weaken the plants and make them more susceptible to disease, so whenever pests are seen or suspected measures should be taken to deal with the trouble.

Aphides are a type of insect pest which attack the flowering cherries. One of the worst offenders is the black cherry aphis which unfortunately does not limit its attack to the edible species. Mealy aphides also trouble the cherries. Often the aphides may only be noticed when sooty moulds are seen upon a sticky substance on the leaves. The aphides exude a honeydew in which the moulds thrive. The honeydew attracts ants so if one sees ants scurrying up and down the branches of shrubs one should always suspect aphides. The ants add to the trouble by carrying female aphides to other shrubs to start new colonies from which they may collect the, to them, delicious honeydew. It is important, therefore, to keep down both aphides and ants.

The aphides may best be controlled by liquid derris which is harmless to animals and humans but deadly to fish; so great care must be taken not to let the spray drift on to lily-pools or tubs containing goldfish.

Liquid derris in a strong solution is also effective against ants, particularly if the nests are discovered and sprayed. Ants tend to make their nests under paving or edging stones but they may also be in the open ground. Wherever a strong colony of ants is seen the nest must be sought and exterminated either by derris or one of

176

the proprietary ant-killers—'Nippon' is one which we have found effective.

American Blight or *Woolly Aphis* will be familiar to all who grow apple trees, covering the twigs with a white woolly substance that looks like cotton-wool. A similar aphis sometimes attacks pyracanthas, flowering crabs, mountain ashes, and cotoneasters. The best control is to spray three times at weekly intervals with one quarter of an ounce of liquid nicotine and one quarter of an ounce of soft soap to two gallons of water. *Note.* Nicotine is poisonous to animals and humans and must therefore be used with great care.

Bark Beetles are of two types. One burrows into the actual wood of the stems and branches and is called the shot borer. The other tunnels between the bark and the wood. Flowering cherries, crabs, and hawthorns are most likely to be attacked.

As in the case of many other pests, the weakest trees and shrubs are usually attacked and indeed an overwhelming insect attack on any plant should cause one to look for cultural faults. Perhaps a shrub is being drained and weakened by the roots of a near-by over-greedy feeder. In the case of the bark beetles, waterlogging is the fault which usually leads to their presence. If care is taken to plant only in properly drained soil one should have little trouble from these particular pests. Mulches, too, help a great deal. If the holes of bark beetles are seen, the affected wood must be sawn off and burnt. If the whole shrub is attacked it should be dug up and burnt to prevent the trouble spreading to other shrubs and trees in the garden.

Caterpillars can be very troublesome in the shrub garden. We have had valuable shrubs almost eaten away by the caterpillars and capsid bugs from near-by fruit trees. Caterpillars of the lackey moth, vapourer moth, winter moth, small ermine moth, and tortoise moth are also liable to cause damage. Where leaves have been eaten, the shrubs should be examined in winter when the eggs may be seen and burnt. Spraying with liquid derris in March and April will give control.

The caterpillar of the leopard moth is an even more serious, but fortunately rarer, pest. It will bore into the branches of a flowering shrub for twelve inches or more, causing the leaves to wilt and the branch to die. If this ever unaccountably happens in your garden look at once for a heap of brown frass at the base of the stem or trunk. This will often lead you to the tunnel up which it should be possible to push a wire and so kill the caterpillar.

Leaf Miners are a type of maggot which tunnel into the foliage making marks in the tissue of the leaves. Lilacs, laburnums, and azaleas are most often attacked. In the case of azaleas the leaves go yellow and shrivel; blisters form on the lilac leaves which then curl; while the laburnum leaves merely become blotched. The grub is usually about an inch long and pale green in colour and may be controlled with a spray of nicotine.

Mealy Bugs are covered by a waxy-white secretion which protects their bodies. They affect the upper and lower surfaces of leaves in colonies rather in the way that scale insects do and infest particularly laburnums, ceanothuses, flowering currants, and robinias. They may be dealt with by spraying in spring with white oil and nicotine in the proportion of half an ounce of liquid nicotine to half a pint of white oil emulsion to five gallons of water. The best results come from spraying in the evening after a warm spring day.

Red Spiders are usually found upon prunus, malus, chaenomeles, or mountain ash, and upon azaleas. If the branches are examined in the winter, particularly at the base of young shoots, the red eggs of the mites may be found. These hatch into tiny, orangey-red mites which feed on the undersides of the leaves near the midrib, sucking the sap and causing the foliage to turn yellow. Attacks of red spider may be controlled in ornamental cherries by spraying just before flowering with a liver of sulphur wash, dissolving half an ounce of soft soap in two gallons of water and stirring in an ounce of liver of sulphur. It is important thoroughly to spray the under-surface of the unfolding leaves. Flowering crabs, mountain ashes, and ornamental quinces should be sprayed with lime sulphur a week before flowering. When azaleas are affected it is safer to dust only with lime sulphur.

Scale Insects form colonies that look like a hard crust on the surface of the leaves. The scales may be brown or white in colour and appear on the upper- and under-surface of the leaves. They should be controlled by a spray of white oil and nicotine in the proportions recommended for mealy bugs.

Weevils eat the leaves of many flowering shrubs, especially those of rhododendrons, buddleias, crab-apples, chaenomeles, and rowans. They may be controlled by liquid derris or derris dust.

White Fly attacks rhododendrons and usually shows itself as a yellow mottling on the upper-surface of the leaves of the hardy hybrids. To gain control of the trouble in the case of severe infestations spray with liquid derris in September, April, and during the summer.

Rhododendron Bug is another pest which concentrates upon the rhododendron genus, causing a marbled effect on the upper-surface of the leaves and a chocolate spotting on the lower-surface. The bugs may usually be seen in June when badly affected leaves should be removed and burnt. 'D.D.T.' powder or a spray of nicotine, soft soap and 'D.D.T.' are the best means of dealing with the pest.

Vine Weevils attack other plants but they are particularly addicted to the early-flowering rhododendrons. The weevils eat the leaves at the edge in an unmistakable kind of pattern. The insect is about a third of an inch long and dull black in colour. It is active in April and May, feeding on the leaves at night and by day hiding in the mulch or in any dead leaves, stones, or rubbish on the ground. Some growers insist on doing away with the mulch as the only means to control the pest. We have, however, been quite successful in combating a heavy attack on the rhododendrons 'Blue Tit', 'Blue Diamond', and 'Humming Bird' (which apparently brought the weevils with them from the nursery when they arrived) by puffing well with 'D.D.T.' powder and renewing the dust after rain. The *Rhododendron Leaf Hopper* which looks like a small grasshopper and appears in late June may be controlled by similar means. This insect makes tiny punctures on the buds and leaf-stems with its nose and is thought to spread the fungus disease of bud blast.

Bud Blast destroys the flower and occasionally the growth-buds of rhododendrons and is particularly prevalent in the south of England. The buds are first discoloured and later go quite black;

minute hairs which are really the spores of the fungus appear on the surface. No cure has yet been found and it is wise to pick off and burn all affected buds and cut back affected growth.

Feeding with sulphate of potash during April, May, and June increases a plant's resistance and this potash is conveniently supplied by mulching with chopped green bracken.

Azaleas, particularly the evergreen varieties, are sometimes subject to a disfiguring blight in which the tips of the stems and terminal leaves and buds become swollen and covered with a white bloom. All affected parts should be immediately cut away and burnt. A lime-sulphur spray (a half a pint to two gallons of water) in January will help to prevent a recurrence of the trouble.

Coral Spot is a fungus which may attack any shrub or tree. First the branch dies from the tip right back to the point of infection. The tiny little pink cushions which give the trouble its name then appear on the dead wood. At the first sign of trouble it is important to cut out all the dead wood and burn it immediately to prevent the spread of the fungus.

Mildew is familiar to most gardeners. It appears particularly on roses, flowering cherries, crabs, hawthorns, firethorns, ornamental quinces, mountain ashes, and indeed all members of the *Rosaceae* family as well as upon Michaelmas daisies and various other plants. 'Karathane' is the most effective means of control I know although simple dusting with flowers of sulphur is remarkably effective.

Shoestring Fungus or *Honey Fungus* is the most dread disease of all. It attacks the roots of shrubs, eventually producing long strands of mycelia which look like black leather shoe-laces. It is usually thought to be incurable and all affected plants should be dug up at once and burnt. I like to burn them in the hole out of which they have been dug where it is possible to do this without fire danger to near-by shrubs. I feel that this burning may help to cleanse the trouble from the soil. In America, however, carbon bisulphide is injected into the soil to a depth of nine inches at eighteen-inch intervals. I feel this is worth trying. Nothing should be neglected which may help to stop the spread of this heart-breaking trouble which may claim the best trees and shrubs in a garden without apparent cause.

PESTS AND DISEASES

Old prunings and dying shrubs or branches help to spread the trouble. Imported leaf-mould from an affected wood may bring it to your garden. That is why I feel that bracken and peat are the safest substances with which to mulch.

On the whole, though, the shrub gardener is little troubled as a rule by pests and diseases. Good cultivation; a high standard of garden hygiene in removing prunings, etc., promptly; regular applications of suitable mulches, and quick action at the first sign of trouble should help to keep your shrubs healthy and unharassed by pests.

In revising this book I would like to draw to the attention of the reader two new remedies: *Benlate* is a systemic fungicide, particularly useful in treating rust, black spot and mildew in roses. *Armillatox* is a remedy for the dreaded honey fungus and has been proved effective when used in time. Wherever die-back or discolouration of leaves occurs in shrubs this disorder should be suspected and the soil around examined for the bootlace-like rhizomorphs. Other symptoms are a thin white sheet of growth under the bark of the collar or roots, often with fan-like striations, black streaks or patches and a strong mushroomy smell.

Armillatox can be used, not only to treat the infected plants, but also for the protection of nearby shrubs and trees and the sterilization of any infected areas.

Lists of Shrubs and Trees Suitable for the Small Garden

CARPETING SHRUBS

Evergreen or Deciduous	Name	Season of Bloom	Height and Spread in feet
E	*Calluna vulgaris* (Ling)	Sept.	2 × 2
E	*Calluna v.* 'Alportii'	Aug. and Sept.	$1\frac{1}{2}$ × 2
E	*Calluna v.* 'Flore Pleno'	Oct.	2 × 2
E	*Calluna v.* 'Goldsworth Crimson'	Aug. and Sept.	$2\frac{1}{2}$ × 2
E	*Calluna v.* 'Hammondii'	Sept. and Oct.	2 × 2
E	*Calluna v.* 'H.E. Beale'	Aug. and Sept.	3 × 2
E	*Calluna v.* 'J.H. Hamilton'	Aug. and Sept.	2 × 2
E	*Cytisus × kewensis*	April to May	1 × 4
E	*Daboecia*	June to Oct.	2 × 3
E	*Daphne blagayana*	Feb.	1 × 3
E	*Erica carnea* 'Eileen Porter'	Nov. to Feb.	$\frac{1}{2}$ × $\frac{3}{4}$
E	*Erica carnea* 'James Backhouse'	Late Jan. to March	$\frac{3}{4}$ × $1\frac{1}{2}$
E	*Erica carnea* 'King George'	Jan. to March	$\frac{3}{4}$ × $1\frac{1}{2}$
E	*Erica carnea* 'Praecox'	Late Jan. to March	$\frac{3}{4}$ × $1\frac{1}{2}$
E	*Erica carnea* 'Ruby Glow'	Late Feb. to April	$\frac{1}{2}$ × $1\frac{1}{2}$

182

LIST OF SHRUBS

E	*Erica carnea* 'Springwood'	Late Jan. to March	$\frac{1}{2} \times 2$
E	*Erica carnea* 'Springwood Pink'	Late Jan. to March	$1\frac{1}{2} \times 1\frac{1}{2}$
E	*Erica carnea* 'Vivelli'	Late Feb. to April	$\frac{1}{2} \times 1$
E	*Erica carnea* 'Winter Beauty'	Dec. to March	$\frac{3}{4} \times 1\frac{1}{2}$
E	*Erica ciliaris* and varieties	June to Nov.	1×2
E	*Erica cinerea* and varieties	July and Aug.	$1 \times 1\frac{1}{2}$
E	*Erica* × *darleyensis*	Jan. to April	$1\frac{1}{2} \times 2$
E	*Erica* × *darleyensis* 'Arthur Johnson'	Dec. to April	$1\frac{1}{2} \times 2$
E	*Erica mediterranea* 'W.T. Rackliff'	Feb. to March	2×3
E	*Erica tetralix*	June to Oct.	$1\frac{1}{2} \times 2$
E	*Erica tetralix* 'Alba mollis'	June to Oct.	$1 \times 1\frac{1}{2}$
E	*Erica vagans* and varieties	July to Oct.	$1\frac{1}{2} \times 3$
E	*Fabiana imbricata* '**Prostrata**'	May to June	1×3
E	*Gaultheria procumbens*	Berries in autumn	$\frac{1}{4} \times 3$
E	*Gaultheria tricophylla*	Berries in autumn	$\frac{1}{4} \times 2$
E	*Genista lydia*	May to June	1×3
E	*Genista pilosa* 'Nana'	May	$1\frac{1}{4} \times 3$
E	*Genista tinctoria* 'Plena'	July	$\frac{1}{2} \times 2$
E	*Helianthemum*	June and Sept.–Oct. (shear in July)	$\frac{1}{2} \times \frac{3}{4}$
E	*Rosmarinus o. lavandulaceus* (hardy only on well-drained bank or rockery in poor soil)	March to April	1×3

DWARF SHRUBS UP TO THREE FEET IN HEIGHT

Evergreen or Deciduous	Name	Season of Interest	Height and Spread in feet
E	Azaleas (evergreen) Kurumé and *malvatica* × *kaempferi* types (some may over a great many years reach five feet in height)	May	3×4
E	Azaleas (evergreen) Gumpos and Ferndown hybrids	June and July	2×2
E	*Cistus* × *corbariensis*	Summer	2×3
E	*Cistus* × *crispus*	May–July	1×2
E	*Cistus* × *skanbergii*	May–June and Sept.	3×3
E	*Cytisus* × *beanii*	May	1×2
E	*Cytisus hirsutus*	April–August	2×2
E	*Cytisus* × *kewensis*	April–May	1×4
E	*Cytisus purpureus*	May	2×4
E	*Daphne collina neapolitana*	May and Sept.	$\frac{1}{2} \times 1$
E	*Daphne cneorum*	May	1×2
D	*Forsythia viridissima* 'Bronxensis'	March–April	2×2
E	*Gaultheria cuneata*	Berries in autumn	$1\frac{1}{2} \times 2$
E	*Gaultheria miqueliana*	Berries in autumn	$\frac{3}{4} \times 2$
E	*Genista lydia*	May–June	2×3
D	*Hydrangea* 'Vulcan'	Aug.–Sept.	2×2
E	*Hypericum* × *moserianum* (supposed to be slightly tender but thrives in Derbyshire)	July and Aug.–Sept.	2×3
E	*Kalmia glauca*	May	$1\frac{1}{2} \times 3$
E	*Lavandula spica* 'Nana Alba' (dwarf white lavender)	June	$\frac{1}{2} \times 1$

E	Lavender (Dutch or Old English clipped after flowering)	July	$2\frac{1}{2}\times 3$
E	Lavender 'Munstead dwarf'	June	$1\frac{1}{2}\times 2$
D	*Potentilla mandschurica*	June to Oct.	2×2
E	*Rhododendron repens* hybrids 'Ethel', 'Elizabeth', 'Jenny', 'Little Bert', etc.		2×2
E	*Rosmarinus* 'Severn Sea'	April–May	2×2
E	*Sarcococca humilis*	Jan.–Feb.	$1\frac{1}{2}\times 3$
E	*Veronicas* 'Autumn Glory' and 'Bowles Hybrid'	Aug.–Nov.	2×2
D	*Viburnum farreri* 'Nanum'	Nov.–March	$1\frac{1}{2}\times 2$

SHRUBS THREE FEET TO FIVE FEET IN HEIGHT

D	*Acer palmatum* 'Dissectum Atropurpureum'	Purple leaf from April to frost	3×3
E	*Berberis* × *stenophylla* 'Irwinii' and other varieties	April and May	3×3
D	*Berberis wilsonae*	Berries and autumn colour	3×3
E	*Carpenteria californica*	July	4×6
D	*Chaenomeles* 'Knap Hill Scarlet' and 'Boule de Feu'	April	5×6
D	*Chaenomeles speciosa* 'Simonii'	April	3×6
E	*Cistus villosus*	May–July	4×3
D	*Corylopsis pauciflora*	March	4×5
E	*Cotoneaster conspicuus* 'Decorus'	Berries	3×5
E	*Cotoneaster microphyllus*	Crimson berries in winter	3×5

E	*Cytisus* X 'Porlock'	March–April	4 X 4
D	*Cytisus* X *praecox*	April–May	4 X 4
E	*Daphne hybrida (dauphinii)*	Dec. to March–April	3 X 3
D	*Daphne mezereum* and its white variety *D. m.* 'Alba'	Feb. or earlier to April	2 X 3
E	*Desfontainea spinosa*	July and Aug.	4 X 4
D	*Deutzia* (in variety)	June	4 X 5
E	*Escallonia edinensis*	June–July	4 X 4
D	*Forsythia ovata*	Feb.–March	4 X 4
D	*Fuchsia* 'Mme Cornellison'	July–Oct.	4 X 3
D	*Fuchsia* 'Mrs. Popple'	July–Oct.	4 X 3
D	*Fuchsia magellanica* 'Alba'	July–Oct.	3 X 4
D	*Fuchsia magellanica* 'Riccartonii'	July–Oct.	4 X 4
E	*Hebe (Veronica) salicifolia*	July–Nov.	4 X 5
D	*Hippophae rhamnoides*	Foliage and berries	6 X 5
D	Hydrangea (lacecap varieties)	July–Sept.	$3\frac{1}{2}$ X 5
D	*Hypericum* 'Hidcote'	July–Oct.	4 X 3
E	*Kalmia angustifolia*	June	3 X 3
E	*Lupinus arboreus*	June	4 X 6
D	*Magnolia stellata* (will reach ten feet in height after many years)	March and April	4 X 3
E	*Mahonia aquifolium*	March	3 X 4
E	*Pernettya mucronata* Davis's hybrids	Large coloured berries	2 X 2
D	*Philadelphus microphyllus*	May–June	3 X 3
D	*Potentilla fruticosa* 'Buttercup'	June–Oct.	3 X 2
D	*Prunus tenella* 'Fire Hill Form'	March	3 X 5
E	Rhododendrons of the Lapponicum series and hybrids ('Blue Diamond'		

E	Rhododendrons— and 'Augfast' may reach five feet in time but can be kept to a lower height)	April–May	3×4
	williamsianum hybrids 'Dormouse', 'Bow Bells', 'Humming Bird', etc.	April–May	3–4×4
D	*Rosa chinensis* and varieties	May–Nov.	4×4
E	*Senecio greyi*	Grey foliage	4×4
E	*Skimmia japonica* 'Foremanii'	Scarlet berries all winter	4×5
D	*Spiraea arguta*	April–May	6×6
D	*Spiraea bumalda*	Aug.	3×4
D	*Symphoricarpus* 'Magic Berry'	Autumn and winter	3×3
D	*Symphoricarpus racemosus* 'White Hedge'	Autumn and winter	3×5
E	*Thuja* 'Rheingold'	Conifer	4×2
E	*Viburnum davidii*	Turquoise berries in autumn	3×4

SHRUBS FIVE FEET TO EIGHT FEET IN HEIGHT

D	*Acer palmatum* 'Atropurpureum'	Foliage plant	7×5
E	Azalea (deciduous species and hybrids)	May–June	7×5
E	*Berberis aggregata*	Berries in autumn	5×4
E	*Berberis linearifolia*	April flowers	6×4
E	*Berberis × lologensis*	April flowers	6×4
E	*Berberis × stenophylla*	May flowers	7×5
D	*Berberis thunbergii*	Autumn colour	5×5
E	*Camellia (japonica* varieties)	March–April	5×5

E	*Camellia* × *williamsii* varieties	Jan.–April	6×4
E	*Ceanothus* 'A.T. Johnson'	May and Sept.	6×5
E	*Ceanothus* 'Autumnal Blue'	May and Sept.	6×5
E	*Ceanothus* × *burkwoodii*	May and Sept.	5×5
E	*Ceanothus* 'Dignity'	May and Sept.	6×5
D	*Ceanothus* 'Gloire de Versailles' and other deciduous varieties	Aug. and Sept.	6×6
E	*Ceanothus* × *veitchianus*	May	7×6
D	*Chaenomeles* 'Knap Hill Scarlet', 'Boule de Feu', 'Aurora', 'Apple Blossom', etc. (will reach this height against a wall)	April	5×6
E	*Choisya ternata* (shelter from wind; wall in bleak districts)	May and Sept.	5×5
E	*Cistus cyprius* (good drainage)	May–June	6×6
E	*Cistus ladaniferus* (good drainage)	May–June	6×6
E	*Cistus* × *purpureus* (good drainage)	May–June	5×5
D	*Clethra alnifolia*	August	6×5
D	*Clethra barbinervis* (tender)	August	6×5
D	*Cornus alba* 'Spaethii'	Foliage	7×6
E	*Coronilla glauca*	May–Nov.	6×4
D	*Cotoneaster horizontalis*	Scarlet berries	5×8
E	*Cytisus multiflorus* (white Portugal broom)	May	6×4
E	*Cytisus nigricans*	Aug.	6×5
E	*Elaeagnus pungens* 'Maculata'	Variegated evergreen foliage	6×6

E	*Erica arborea* 'Alpina'	April	5×6
E	*Erica lusitanica*		
	(milder districts only)	Feb. to April	7×6
E	*Erica × veitchii*	April	7×6
E	*Escallonia*		
	'Donard Brilliance'	June–July	6×6
E	*Escallonia × iveyi*	June–July	6×5
E	*Escallonia macrantha*	June and Nov.	7×5
E	*Escallonia*		
	'Slieve Donard'	June–July	7×6
D	*Forsythia suspensa* and *F. s.*		
	atrocaulis (must be hard-		
	pruned after flowering)	March–April	5×4
E	*Garrya elliptica*	Catkins in January	7×5
D	*Hamamelis mollis*	Jan. and Feb.	7×7
E	*Hebe speciosa* (*Veronica*)	July–Nov.	5×5
D	*Hoheria lyallii*	July–Aug.	6×10
D	*Hydrangea hortensia*		
	(most varieties)	July to Sept.	5×5
D	*Hydrangea paniculata*	Aug.	6×6
D	*Hypericum* 'Rowallane'	July–Oct.	5×3
E	*Ilex a.* 'Golden King'	Holly berries	6×5
D	*Indigofera gerardiana* and		
	hebepetala (slightly		
	tender)	July	5×3
D	*Jasminum nudiflorum*		
	(winter jasmine)		
	(scrambling shrub)	Nov. to March	6×6
E	*Juniperus squamata*		
	'Meyeri'	Conifer	6×8
E	*Kalmia latifolia*	June	5×4
E	*Leptospermum* 'Chapmanii'	June and Nov.	7×5
	(tender shrub)		
E	*Leptospermum* 'Nicholsii'		
	(tender shrub)	June and Nov.	7×5
D	*Lespedeza thunbergii*		
	(usually cut by frost)	Sept.	7×5

D	*Lonicera × purpusii*	Dec. to June	6×6
E	*Mahonia japonica*	Dec. to Feb.	7×5
D	*Philadelphus* 'Albâtre'	June	6×4
D	*Philadelphus* 'Belle Etoile'	June	5×3
D	*Philadelphus* 'Bouquet Blanc'	June	6×3
D	*Philadelphus* 'Virginale'	June	7×7
D	*Potentilla* 'Katherine Dykes'	May–Oct.	5×5
D	*Potentilla vilmoriniana*	June–Oct.	5×3
D	*Prunus incisa*	March	6×5
D	*Prunus incisa* 'February Pink'	Feb.	6×5
D	*Prunus subhirtella* 'Pendula Rosea'	Nov.–April	6×6
E	*Pyracantha rogersiana*	Winter berries	6×5
E	Rhododendrons (hardy hybrids)	May–June	7×7
E	*Rhododendron × praecox* and *mucronulatum*	Jan.–Feb.–March	5×4-5
E	Rhododendrons of the 'Fabia', 'Carita', 'Naomi' and 'Grosclaude' class	May–June	7×7
D	*Romneya coulteri* (wall)	July	5×5
D	*Rosa harisonii*	May	5×3
D	*Rosa primula* (incense rose)	May	6×5
D	*Rosa rugosa* (varieties and hybrids)	May–Oct.	6×6
D	*Rosa* 'Canary Bird'	May	6×6
D	Roses—hybrid musk	Summer and autumn	5×6
E	*Rosmarinus officinalis*	Nov.–May	6×5
D	*Stachyurus praecox*	Feb.–March–April	5×3
D	*Viburnum × bodnantense*	Nov.–April	8×5

LIST OF SHRUBS

D	*Viburnum carlesii*	April	6×6
D	*Viburnum farreri*	Nov.–April	7×5
D	*Viburnum plicatum*	May–June	6×6
D	*Viburnum plicatum* 'Mariesii'	May–June	5×10
D	*Weigela (Diervilla)* (most varieties)	May	5×5

SHRUBS EIGHT FEET IN HEIGHT AND OVER

E	*Acacia dealbata* (warm wall in south and west only)	Feb.–March	20×12
E	*Berberis darwinii*	March–April	8×6
D	*Buddleia alternifolia*	May–June	8×8
D	*Buddleia davidii* and varieties	July–Aug.	8×6
Semi E	*Buddleia globosa*	May	8×6
D	*Chimonanthus praecox*	Dec.–March	8×6
D	*Clethra delavayi* (tender)	July	10×6
D	*Clethra fargesii* (tender)	August	8×6
E	*Coronilla emerus*	May	8×4
D	*Corylopsis spicata*	March	8×8
D	*Corylopsis willmottiae*	March	12×10
D	*Cytisus battandieri*	May–July	10×6
E	*Cytisus scoparius* and hybrids	May–June	8×3
D	*Euonymus alatus*	Spindle berries	8×7
D	*Euonymus europaeus*	Spindle berries	8×8
D	*Forsythia intermedia* 'Spectabilis'	March	8×6
E	*Genista aetnensis*	Aug.	8×6
E	*Genista cinerea*	July–Aug.	8×6
E	*Genista virgata*	June	8×6
D	*Hibiscus syriacus* and varieties	Aug.–Sept.	8×3

E	*Ilex aquifolium:*	
	'J.C. Van Tol',	
	'Argenteomarginata',	
	'Bacciflava ('*Fructoluteo*')	
	and 'Flavescens'	Holly berries	8 × 5
E	*Itea ilicifolia*	Aug. onwards	8 × 8
E	*Pyracantha coccinea*		
	'Lalandii'	Sept. berries	8 × 8
D	*Ribes atrosanguineum*		
	and varieties	March–April	8 × 8
D	*Rosa spinosissima*		
	'Frühlingsgold'	May	8 × 8
E	*Spartium junceum*	Aug.–Nov.	8 × 6
E	*Stranvaesia davidiana*	Berries and autumn	
	salicifolia	colour	8 × 5
D	*Tamarix pentandra*	Aug.	8 × 5
D	*Viburnum opulus* 'Sterile'	May–June	8 × 8

SMALL TREES

D	*Acer griseum*	Foliage and bark
		(year round)	15 × 8
D	*Acer* 'Heptalobum	Spring, summer, and
	Elegans'	autumn foliage	8 × 6
D	*Acer* 'Osakazuki'	Spring, summer, and
		autumn foliage	7 × 5
D	*Amelanchier canadensis*	April flowers and
		autumn colour	10 × 8
E	*Azara microphylla* (not	
	hardy in cold districts)	Feb.	10 × 6
D	*Cercis siliquastrum*	May (autumn colour)	10 × 6
E	*Chamaecyparis l.* 'Fletcheri'	Foliage	12 × 5
E	*Chaemaecyparis l.* 'Lutea'	Golden foliage	15 × 6
E	*Chamaecyparis l.* 'Pembury	
	Blue'	Bluish foliage	15 × 8
E	*Chamaecyparis l.* 'Stewartii'	
	(not as good as *C. lutea*	
	for colour when adult)	Golden foliage	15 × 6

LIST OF SMALL TREES

Semi E *Cotoneaster* 'Cornubia'	Winter berries	15 × 12
E *Embothrium lanceolatum* (shelter. 'Norquinço Valley Form' is hardy south of Trent and west)	May	25 × 12
E *Eucalyptus niphophila* (Snow Gum)	Slow growing. Can be kept pruned to required size	12 × 6
D *Eucryphia glutinosa*	August	7 × 6
E *Eucryphia* 'Nymansay' (may reach forty feet in time)	Aug.	20 × 8
E *Juniperus communis* 'Hibernica' (slim pillar-like growth)	Form and foliage year round	7 × 2
D *Laburnum × alpinum*	May	25 × 18
D *Laburnum × vossii*	Later May	15 × 15
D *Laburnum watereri*	Later May	15 × 15
D *Magnolia × highdownensis*	Flowers in May	8 × 8–10
D *Magnolia × s.* 'Alexandrina' (*soulangiana* group)	April	10 × 6
D *Magnolia × s.* 'Lennei' (*soulangiana* group)	May	10 × 6
D *Magnolia × s.* 'Rustica' Rubra' (*soulangiana* group)	May	10 × 6
D *Magnolia sieboldii*	June	8 × 10
D *Magnolia sinensis* (spreading)	June	8 × 8
D *Magnolia × soulangiana*	April	10 × 8
D *Magnolia wilsonii* (best of the June group for limited space)	June	8 × 5
D *Malus atrosanguinea*	May	20 × 12
D *Malus floribunda*	May	20 × 12

D *Prunus × blireiana*		
(red or purple leafed)	March	12×6
D *Prunus cerasifera* 'Nigra'		
(red or purple leafed)	April	20×6
D *Prunus* 'Amanogawa'	April	15×3
Prunus 'Kiku-Shidare		
Sakura'	April	8×6
Prunus 'Shimidsu		
Sakura'	May	12×8
D *Prunus serrulata* 'Fugenzo'		
('J.H. Veitch')	April–May	15×10
D *Prunus serrulata*		
'Oshukun'	April–May	15×8
D *Prunus serrulata*		
'Pink Perfection'	April–May	12×8
D *Prunus serrulata* 'Ukon'	April	15×10
D *Prunus subhirtella*		
'Autumnalis'	Nov.–March	15×10
D *Prunus subhirtella*		
'Beni Higan'	March	15×8
D *Prunus × yedoensis*		
'Shidare Yoshino'		
(weeping)	March–April	15×8
D *Pyrus salicifolia* 'Pendula'		
(silver-leafed weeping		
pear)	March–April	8×6
D *Sorbus aucuparia*	Scarlet berries	
(mountain ash)	Sept.–Oct.	15×8
D *Sorbus hupehensis*	White berries in autumn	12×5
E *Tricuspidaria lanceolata*		
(shelter or wall)	June	10×8

RECENT SHRUB INTRODUCTIONS
FOR THE SMALL GARDEN

Berberis thunbergii 'Aurea'
Berberis thunbergii 'Rose Glow'

Golden-foliaged forms of *Calluna vulgaris* (Ling), particularly:
  'Gold Haze'
  'Joy Vanstone'
  'Orange Queen'
  'Robert Chapman'
  'Sunset'
Ceanothus thyrsiflorus repens (mound-forming carpeter—bright blue flowers)
C. t. 'Southmead' (medium-sized shrub)
Cotoneaster conspicuus 'Decorus' (low-growing—useful to cover dry banks)
C. conspicuus 'Highlight' (medium-size—arching growth)
Ground-covering cotoneasters:
C. salicifolius 'Autumn Fire' (small to medium—semi-weeping habit)
C. s. 'Parkteppich' (partially prostrate)
C.s. 'Repens' (prostrate—excellent ground-cover)
Genista tinctoria 'Royal Gold' (small free-flowering broom)
Helichrysum italicum (syn. *H. rupestre*), good silver-foliaged plant, needing sharp drainage and full sun
H. splendidum (leaves grey-white, flowers bright yellow)
Particularly distinctive and decorative hydrangeas:
H. 'Ayesha'
H. heteromalla 'Snowcap' (very hardy and stands most exposures)
H. 'Preziosa'
Potentilla 'Minstead Dwarf' (yellow)
P. 'Sunset' (orange to brick-red flowers)
P. 'Tangerine' (soft coppery yellow)
Salix hastata 'Wehrhahnii' (small shrub with silvery catkins turning to yellow)
S. lapponum (small grey willow with silky catkins in early spring)
Spiraea nipponica tosaensis (June-flowering)
Viburnum 'Anne Russell' (very fragrant *carlesii* cross)
V. carlesii 'Aurora' (pink flowered cultivar of great charm)
V. plicatum 'Pink Beauty' (white lace-caps becoming pink as they age)
V. tinus 'Eve Price' (compact form of laurustinus with pink-tinged flowers)

RECENT SHRUB INTRODUCTIONS

CONIFERS

Chamaecyparis lawsoniana 'Chilworth Silver' (broadly columnar)

C. l. 'Columnaris' (narrowly conical, glaucous tipped)

C. l. 'Winston Churchill' (gold foliage—medium size)

C. pisifera 'Boulevard' (medium shrub—steel blue foliage, purple tinged in winter)

Ground-covering junipers:

Juniperus communis 'Effusa' (wide spreading—semi prostrate)

J. horizontalis 'Bar Harbor' (glaucous, ground-hugging carpeter)

J. h. 'Wiltonii' (glaucous blue carpeter)

Some Useful Addresses

Dwarf Heaths and Inexpensive Popular Shrubs
  Messrs. Jas. Smith and Sons, Darley Dale Nurseries, Darley
  Dale, Derbyshire.
Rhododendrons, Azaleas, and General Shrubs and Trees
  Messrs. Hilliers, Winchester, Hants.
  Messrs. G. Reuthe Ltd., Keston, Kent.
Azaleas and Hardy Hybrid Rhododendrons
  Messrs. Knap Hill Nurseries, Lower Knap Hill, Woking,
  Surrey.
  Messrs. Hydon Nurseries, Hydon Heath, Surrey.
Shrub Roses and Rose Species
  Murrells of Shrewsbury, Portland Nurseries,
  Shrewsbury.
Herbaceous and Underplantings
  W. E. Th. Ingwersen Ltd., Birch Farm Nursery, Gravetye,
  East Grinstead, Sussex.
  Margery Fish Nurseries, East Lambrook Manor, South
  Petherton, Somerset.
  Messrs. Perry, Hardy Plant Farm, Enfield, Middlesex.
Herbaceous Plants and Bulbs
  Messrs. Wallace and Barr, The Nurseries, Marden, Kent.
Bulbs
  Messrs. Walter Blom, Leavesden, Watford, Herts.
Virus-resistant, Ultra-hardy Lilies
  Cheshire Bulb Farms Ltd., 10 Maynestone Road, Chinley,
  via Stockport, Cheshire.
Water Plants and Streamside Plantings
  Messrs. Perry, Hardy Plant Farm, Enfield, Middlesex.

ADDRESSES

Royal Horticultural Society
Vincent Square, London SW1 (Minimum subscription –£4.50
single, £7.00 double. Shows, Monthly Journal, Free Seed
Distribution, Advice, Library, Lectures and Meetings.)
Armillatox
Armillatox Ltd., Old Smugglers, Henley, Fernhurst,
Haslemere, Surrey.

Index

INDEX

INDEX

INDEX

INDEX

INDEX

INDEX

J

Jasminum nudiflorum, 21, 115, 149, 189
Jasminum officinale, 148
Jasminum officinale 'Affine', 149
Jasminum polyanthum, 149
Jasminum primulinum, 149
Judas tree, 56
Junipers, 22
Juniperus communis 'Hibernica', 18, 193
Juniperus squamata 'Meyeri', 22–3, 189

K

Kalmia angustifolia 'Rubra', 97, 186
Kalmia glauca, 97, 184
Kalmia latifolia, 97, 189
Kalmia latifolia 'Myrtifolia', 97
Karathane, 76

L

Laburnum alpinum, 55, 193
Laburnum × *vossii,* 55, 193
Laburnum × *watereri,* 55, 193
Lavatera olbia 'Rosea', 15
Lavender, 18, 22, 185
Lavender dwarf, 44, 184, 185
Lavendula spica, 94, 185
Lavendula spica 'Nana Alba', 94, 184
Layering, 172, 173
Layering, air, 173
Leaf Miners, 178
Leaf Mould, 16
Lenten roses – see *Helleborus*
   orientalis hybrids
Leptospermum scoparium 'Chapmanii', 95, 189

Leptospermum scoparium 'Nichollsii', 95, 189
Leptospermum scoparium 'Splendens', 95
Lespedeza thunbergii, 109, 189
Leucojum vernum, 131
Lilacs, 18 (see also *Syringa*)
Lilies, 22
Lilium candidum, 142
Lilium croceum, 142
Lilium × *dalhansonii,* 142
Lilium davidii, 142
Lilium giganteum, 142
Lilium hansonii, 142
Lilium henryi, 142, 143
Lilium martagon, 142
Lilium martagon album, 143
Lilium × *maxwill,* 142
Lilium monadelphum, 142
Lilium pardalinum, 142
Lilium pomponium, 142, 143
Lilium pyrenaicum, 142, 143
Lilium regale, 142, 143
Lilium speciosum, 143
Lilium × *testaceum,* 142–3
Lilium tigrinum, 143
Lilium umbellatum, 142, 143
Lilium willmottiae, 143
Lime haters, 150, 152
Linum narbonense, 128
Lithospermum, 44, 45, 128
Lithospermum rosmarinifolium, 118
Loam, 150
Lonicera × *brownii* 'Fuchsoides', 148
Lonicera etrusca, 147
Lonicera fragrantissima, 116
Lonicera × *grata,* 147
Lonicera periclymenum 'Serotina'
   (Late Dutch), 47
Lonicera × *purpusii,* 116, 190
Lonicera × *standishii,* 116
Lonicera × *tellmanniana,* 148
Lonicera tragophylla, 148
Lupins, tree (*Lupinus arboreus*), 15, 99 186

INDEX

INDEX

INDEX